The Collector's Guide to

PAPERWEIGHTS

FOREWORD

Paperweights are objects of endless fascination. When, in 1954, ex-King Farouk's collection of paperweights was sold in Cairo, considerable publicity was given to the price of French nineteenth-century paperweights, and many people became aware of them and started collections.

A Collector's Guide to Paperweights is a distillation of the research that has been done in the increasingly popular field of paperweight collecting since then. The introduction sets out clearly and lucidly the history of paperweight-making and its origins in the manufacturing of glass, while the main part of the book describes the histories and paperweight-production of the famous French factories of Baccarat, St Louis and Clichy and also of the best antique British and American factories. It then goes on to consider some of the finest collections assembled and the people who put them together.

Sara Rossi is continuing a tradition which has not, until recently, always been acknowledged: that of the dealer who has become a recognized authority on her subject. I recommend this book to the expert and the curious alike.

ANTHONY SPINK
SPINK & SON LTD

The Collector's Guide to

PAPERWEIGHTS

SARA ROSSI

BRACKEN BOOKS

To Luke, Saskia and Nadine

The Collector's Guide to Paperweights

This edition first published in 1995 by Bracken Books,
an imprint of Random House UK Ltd,
Random House, 20 Vauxhall Bridge Road,
London SW1V 2SA

Reprinted 1996

ISBN 1 85891 243 1

Printed and bound in Singapore

ACKNOWLEDGEMENTS

The author and publishers would especially like to thank Titus and
Magdaleine Kendall for their encouragement and support. Grateful thanks also to
Melanie Gibson, Lady Arthur, Sam Aschuler, Manny Davidson, Mr Manny Lacher, Mr and
Mrs Evan Pancake, Lynne Stair, Lauren Tarshis and the Hon. Vincent Weir.

The extract from *Pack My Bag* by Henry Green on page 84 is reprinted by kind permission of Chatto & Windus and The Hogarth Press.

The publishers wish to thank the following individuals and organizations for supplying photographs:

Courtesy of the Bergstrom Mahler Museum, Neenah, Wisconsin: 16 (left) accession no. 112, E H Bergstrom Bequest: 17 (above left) accession no. 340, E H Bergstrom Bequest: 39 accession no. 22, E H Bergstrom Bequest: 61 (above left) accession no. 160, E H Bergstrom Bequest: 61 (above right) accession no. 1A, E H Bergstrom Bequest: 61 (below) accession no. 1253, purchase; 62 accession no. 372, E H Bergstrom Bequest: 63 (above left) accession 1790, gift of Mrs Virginia B Trowbridge: 63 (above right) accession no. 399, E H Bergstrom Bequest: 67 accession no. 130, E H Bergstrom Bequest: 70 (left) accession no. 159, E H Bergstrom Bequest: 71 (right) accession no. 275, E H Bergstrom Bequest: 73 (below left) accession no. 485, E H Bergstrom Bequest: 75 (left) accession no. 99, E H Bergstrom Bequest: 75 (right) accession no. 1458, purchase and gift of Mr & Mrs D J Wiiken: 76 accession no. 132, E H Bergstrom Bequest: 78 accession no. 161, E H Bergstrom Bequest: 79 (right) accession no. 555, E H Bergstrom Bequest: 87 (right) accession no. 357, E H Bergstrom Bequest.

Courtesy of Christie's, © Christie's Colour Library: 7 (below right); 31 (right); 35 (above left); 41; 42; 46; 48 (left); 50; 85; 87 (above right); 88; 89.

Courtesy of the Corning Museum of Glass, Corning, New York: 14, gift of Clara S Peck: 15 (left) gift of Cristalleries de Baccarat: 17 (above right) gift of Hon. & Mrs Amory Houghton: 17 (below left) gift of Hon. & Mrs Amory Houghton: 18 (below left) gift of Clara S Peck (weight) and Victor Lutz (flowers): 18 (below right) gift of Hon. & Mrs Amory Houghton: 19 (above left) gift of Hon. & Mrs. Amory Houghton: 19 (above right); gift of Clara S Peck: 23 (below) gift of Hon. & Mrs. Amory Houghton: 32 gift of Hon. & Mrs Amory Houghton: 55; 64; 65 gift of Clara S Peck: 69 gift of Hon. & Mrs. Amory Houghton: 70 (right); 71 (left); 72 gift of Clara S Peck: 73 (above); 77 (above); 77 (below); 80 (above); 80 (below) gift of Hon. & Mrs Amory Houghton: 84; 87 (left).

Courtesy of Leo Kaplan Ltd: 56.

Courtesy of Mr E Lacher: 57 (above); 68; 74; 79 (left).

Courtesy of Mr & Mrs E Pancake: 39 (above left); 40 (below); 57 (below); 60.

Courtesy of a Private Collection: 81.

Courtesy of Sotheby's London, © Sotheby's Ltd: 7 (below left); 15 (right); 25 (above left and right); 30 (top left); 36 (left); 44; 48 (right); 49 (above); 53 (above).

Courtesy of Sotheby's New York, © 1982 Sotheby's Inc: 54.

Courtesy of Spink & Son Ltd: 6; 7 (top); 8; 9; 10 (left and right); 11; 12; 13; 16 (right); 17 (below right); 21; 22; 23 (above); 24 (left and right); 25 (below); 26 (above and below(; 27 (left and right); 28; 29; 30 (above right, below, left, centre, and right); 31 (left); 33 (above left, above right, and below); 34; 35 (above right, and below); 36 (right); 37 (above and below); 38 (left and right); 39 (above right, and below); 40 (above); 43; 45; 47; 49 (below left, and right); 51; 52; 53 (below); 63 (below); 82; 83.

Publisher's note

Prices for paperweights sold at specific auctions are given in the local currency with the date of sale. All other prices are given in £ sterling followed by US$ in parentheses; the exchange rate has been calculated at £0.606 to US$1.

CONTENTS

INTRODUCTION

A St Louis crown, 1845–60
The five separate colour combinations in the
twists make this an extremely rare weight.

Paperweights are intriguing objects to look at: the longer you examine them, the more you see. These glass objects have aroused a lot of interest over the years, probably more so now than ever before. With prices rising all the time for pieces that combine rarity with the best quality, more and more people are becoming curious and discovering the fascination and charm of paperweights, both antique and modern.

It is marvellous to examine some of the work produced, especially that of the French factories. The flower weights, whether they are natural or stylized, are beautifully produced and portrayed. The complexity of some of the millefiori designs means that they need to be admired at first hand to appreciate the accuracy and skill that must have been required to make them. The intricate designs in many of the weights are so tiny it is hard to comprehend how these internal patterns, whose components are often no bigger than a millimetre across, can be so clearly delineated and so precisely arranged.

Paperweights are a joy to collect for many reasons. They are a relatively small art form, easy to keep, easy to transport and, most importantly of all, they look good with everything. They are compatible with every period and not just works of art from the Victorian period. Paperweights can serve as a pretty complement to furniture, textiles, pictures, clocks and boxes, and yet they look just as good arranged on their own, either in a cabinet or on a flat surface.

Always buy the best paperweights that you can afford and, most importantly, the weights that appeal the most to you. Choose paperweights of good quality and good condition. The wonderful thing about collecting paperweights is that all the different designs are compatible with each other. Some collectors like to collect just flowers, or just magnums or concentrics, but whatever your choice there are really no limitations apart from price.

However, if you want to build up a representative collection that will hold, and with any luck increase, its value then it will be desirable to acquire certain examples of paperweights typical of particular factories such as a swirl from Clichy, a pansy from Baccarat and a crown from St Louis.

Without doubt, the antique French paperweights are the best. No other factories from anywhere else have ever really captured the beauty and potential of glass paperweights so successfully and with so much charm. The classic period of paperweight production, from around 1845 to 1860, is definitely the most beautiful and collectable.

INTRODUCTION

A St Louis dahlia, 1845–60
*This large flower **(left)** comprises five overlapping rows of pink ribbed petals with a central cane of blue, yellow and white. The flower is set upon five green leaf tips, and the base is generously star-cut. Diameter: 2⅞in (7.3cm)*

*A Baccarat 'bouquet de marriage' mushroom, 1845–60 The upward-rising tuft of the mushroom **(below far left)** comprises three rows of stardust canes with green centres around a central red, white and blue arrowhead cluster. It is surrounded by a blue and white torsade. Diameter: 3in (7.6cm)*

*A Clichy rose, 1845–60 This rare example of a large, pink Clichy rose **(left)** is set in clear glass. In addition to the rose, there are a bud, seven green leaves and a stem. Diameter: 2½in (6.3cm)*

7

A St Louis upright bouquet, 1845–60
This tight grouping of flowers, canes and leaves is surrounded by a red and white torsade (left). The glass is faceted with six oval printies around the side and a circular printy on top.

A Clichy mushroom, 1845–60
The mushroom head is set as a concentric (right) with a pink Clichy rose in the middle. The mushroom is encased in clear glass cut with six oval side printies and a circular top printy. Diameter: 2½in (6.3cm)

This book offers beginners and enthusiasts alike the opportunity to enrich their appreciation and understanding of paperweights. By no means a comprehensive encyclopedia, it nonetheless includes a brief history of glass-making, and detailed information about the most significant paperweight-producing factories. Judiciously selected photographs—while no substitute for the real thing—illustrate the features to look out for, as well as celebrating the diversity and splendour that distinguish the finest examples. The Buyer's Guide at the back of the book is meant to offer just that—a guide to the rarity and value of different types of weights. However, the basis of your collection should be one of enjoyment and not of investment, since paperweights are best appreciated if you look at them for what they are—works of art.

A BRIEF HISTORY OF GLASS PAPERWEIGHTS

Glass paperweights in the form that we now recognize them were first produced by factories in Venice, Bohemia-Silesia and, most famously, France in the mid-nineteenth century. Relatively inexpensive to manufacture, they were initially something of a sideline, and for this reason few records exist of the quantity, quality or method of production. Much of the history of glass paperweights up to 1845 is, therefore, a matter of educated conjecture. In 1845, the Venetian glass-maker Pietro Bigaglia and the French glassworks of St Louis each produced a dated paperweight, the quality of which suggest that glass paperweights were probably first made some two or three years earlier. However, some of the techniques involved and the designs employed are many centuries old.

Millefiori is the name given to perhaps the most typical design of paperweights, in which hundreds of coloured glass canes are gathered together in a magnifying, clear glass dome. Millefiori is an Italian word first used in the nineteenth century, whose literal meaning is 'a thousand flowers', but the design dates back to ancient Egypt. In the thirteenth century BC, the Egyptians were making beads from coloured glass rods, and by the second century BC mosaics were being made in which glass rods of different colours were heated up and bound together to form a crude form of millefiori cane. Three or four centuries later, Alexandria and other parts of the Roman Empire were producing glass bowls whose patterns were formed by millefiori canes; examples of this can be seen today in museums including the Corning Museum of Glass in New York and the Victoria and Albert Museum in London. While there is no smooth chronology leading from second-century Rome to nineteenth-century

A Baccarat wheatflower, 1845–60
This magnificent weight comprises a yellow wheatflower
with a stem and eleven green leaves, above which hovers a
brightly-coloured butterfly.
Diameter: 3in (7.6cm)

A Baccarat pansy, 1845–60
This is typical of pansy weights made by Baccarat, with
two large, dark purple petals above three smaller, yellow
and purple petals.
Diameter: 3in (7.6cm)

France, it is important and intriguing to note that the design and technique of producing millefiori glass pre-date paperweight manufacture by some two thousand years.

GLASS-MAKING IN VENICE c.1100–1800

The history and development of glass production over the next thousand years is little known, but by the twelfth century the centre for glass production was Venice. Indeed, there were so many factories that the threat of fire became of great concern to the city, and the factories were persuaded to move to the nearby island of Murano. Glass-makers of the time were held in great esteem, and this was only increased by the move to Murano: the mystery and secrecy surrounding the manufacture of glass could only be enhanced by the setting up of an elite community on an island.

However, during the thirteenth century, the glass-makers' Guild ruled that Venetian glass workers—who had previously been forbidden from taking their skills elsewhere on pain of death—could travel to other countries to find employment, and their secret skills were rapidly disseminated as far as England and Bohemia. With Murano's reputation in jeopardy it is perhaps not surprising that Venetian glass-makers should begin experimenting with new, or revived, techniques, and despite competition, particularly from the glassworks of Bohemia-Silesia, Venice remained a centre of excellence for glass production over the next

five hundred years. In the fifteenth century, records kept by Marcantonio Sabellico, the librarian of St Mark's Cathedral, indicate that the technique of millefiori was again being used in Venetian glassware. Latticinio was being produced in abundance from the late-sixteenth century onwards, and during the eighteenth century a family named Miotti perfected the technique of aventurine. However, by the end of the eighteenth century, Venetian dominance was truly on the wane: fewer than four hundred glass-makers were still working on Murano; the secret of aventurine had died out with the Miotti family; and Giuseppe Briati, the last Venetian to specialize in latticinio glass, had died in 1772, taking all but a rudimentary knowledge of latticinio manufacture with him.

GLASS-MAKING IN THE NINETEENTH CENTURY AND THE BIRTH OF THE PAPERWEIGHT

The remarkable and sudden appearance of glass paperweights in the 1840s gives rise to the question, when and why was the first paperweight made? Extraordinary as it may seem, the most likely answer is that a number of people all had the same idea of employing old techniques in a new form (the paperweight) at almost exactly the same time.

The secrecy surrounding glass-making means that it is difficult to state all but a few facts with any confidence. What is certain is that one Dr W. E. Fuss of

A St Louis mushroom, signed and dated 'SL 1848'
This is a beautiful weight. In the circle of dark green and pink canes towards the perimeter is a cane bearing the signature and the date. Surrounding the mushroom is a blue and white torsade.
Diameter: 3in (7.6cm)

Silesia was successfully using millefiori in wine glasses, vases and jugs from 1833, and that Pietro Bigaglia in Venice was, with the financial backing of Dal Mistro Barbaria and Co., experimenting with latticinio and aventurine techniques in the 1830s. In France, the glassworks of Baccarat and St Louis were gaining national and international recognition for their fine work in coloured glass, although they were no great innovators, tending instead to imitate and improve upon designs and techniques they saw being used elsewhere. In the early-nineteenth century, probably the finest French glass factory was that of Choisy-le-Roi, whose young director, Georges Bontemps, took an exceptional interest in old Venetian glass-making techniques, and is widely credited with having introduced Italian glass-blowing techniques and the secret of millefiori glass to France. However, it is doubtful whether the factory at Choisy ever manufactured paperweights: the 1848 revolution seriously disrupted business, and three years later the factory was closed down and Bontemps had moved to England.

Paperweights evolved in a curious way: at the end of the day when all the other workers had gone home, glassblowers would experiment using different coloured glass rods to make pretty patterns, encasing them in clear glass to form a small, fairly heavy artefact primarily intended to keep loose papers in place. Clearly these glassblowers must have spent a considerable amount of time investigating and experimenting with the process of manufacture and their techniques were a closely-guarded secret. This makes even more remarkable the virtually simultaneous manufacture of paperweights by some six or seven different sources and the speed with which the process of manufacture was perfected.

THE CLASSIC PERIOD

The classic period for paperweight manufacture—both in terms of quantity and quality—began in about 1842, although few weights were produced much before 1845. The period reached its height in 1851 in France; in the rest of Europe the vogue continued for a further decade, and paperweights continued to find a market in the United States well into the 1870s. By this time, all three of the great French paperweight-making factories had ceased production.

One of the main commercial attractions of paperweights was how economical they were to produce. Not only were they cost-effective, they were also highly saleable as they were so versatile. In the 1840s, they were stocked by stationery shops as useful and decorative writing accessories, and soon the process of paperweight-making was expanded by applying the techniques to waferstands, tazzas, scent bottles, shot glasses and wine glasses.

Paperweights have a calculated interior design, however intricate the pattern. The design is usually set down into the glass near the base, but it is important

A Clichy garlanded posy, 1845–60
Above a bed of horizontal cables sits a white stylized flower. Around the edge is a garland including six large Clichy roses. Diameter: 2³/4in (7cm)

to note that each factory's products have different characteristics. There are, nonetheless, common denominators in particularly fine examples of paper-weights. In close-pack millefioris, the canes should reach right down to the bottom of the glass, whereas flower designs are located away from the base, usually about one-third of the way up the dome. There should always be a generous magnifying dome of clear lead glass over the design and, according to the factory, there is sometimes cutting on the base. Alternatively, other weights have a small cavity where the pontil rod has been removed. Sometimes the clear glass dome is faceted, either in the typical fashion of small cuts all over the surface, or with printies (circular or

oval concave windows cut into the surface of the glass). In more elaborately decorated weights, the surface of the dome that is not cut with printies is embellished with a coloured overlay, and the overlay itself can be decorated with small gilded flowers.

The pre-eminent manufacturers of glass paper-weights during the classic period were three factories from France: two, Baccarat and St Louis, were situated

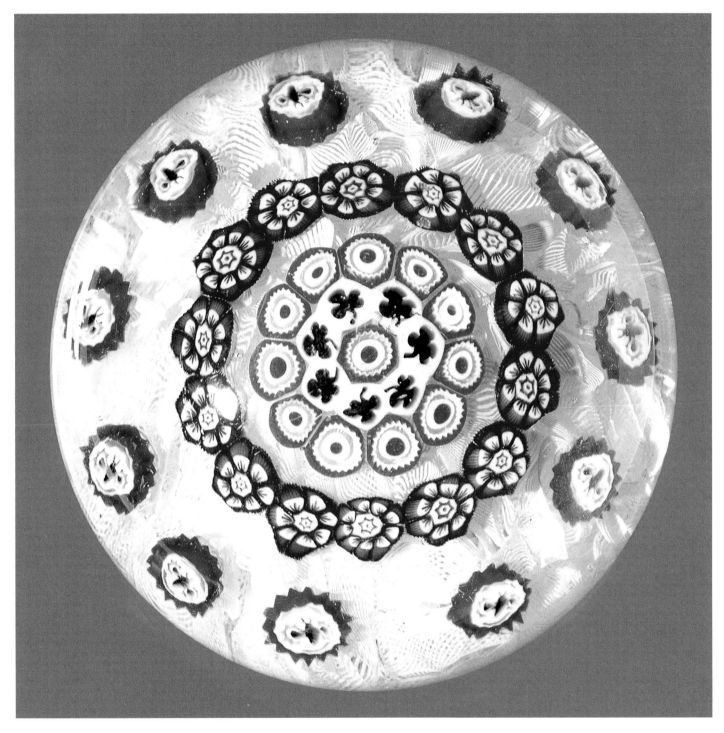

A Baccarat special pattern, 1845–60
This rare weight includes eleven green butterfly canes and
seven green shamrock canes.
Diameter: 3in (7.6cm)

in Alsace-Lorraine, and the third, Clichy, in a suburb of Paris. Further information about each of these can be found in later sections of the book. By the late 1840s, not even the efforts of Pietro Bigaglia could save Venice's declining reputation. Bigaglia's first dated paperweight was made in 1845 and was exhibited at the Austrian Industrial Fair of the same year. Eugene Peligot, a representative of the Paris Chamber of Commerce, saw the weight at the Fair, and returned to France believing that paperweights could well revive the ailing French glass industry. The fact that St Louis produced a dated paperweight in the same year suggests that others had had the same idea somewhat earlier, but Bigaglia remains credited as perhaps the father of the glass paperweight. However, Venetian paperweights lacked the sophistication and refinement of those being produced in Bohemia-Silesia, Britain and France: the colours of the canes were crude; the patterns somewhat random; and the glass domes were sometimes cloudy and rough-finished, and they failed to magnify the internal designs. By 1852, Venetian glass paperweight-making had ceased.

THE MAKING OF A PAPERWEIGHT

A Clichy melon-ribbed overlay, 1845–60
Inside the weight is a basket of millefiori.
Note the Clichy rose on top.

I n order to appreciate and enjoy the composition and design of paperweights, it is important to understand the basic elements and chemistry of glass-making.

Glass was invented by at least 3000 BC. It was first made from a mixture of silica (silicon-dioxide-2), lime (which is impervious to the effects of water), and another alkali such as potash or soda (to facilitate the melting of the batch). When this substance is heated, the mixture becomes soft and malleable. As the melted glass begins to cool, it can be formed by a variety of techniques into a vast array of shapes and sizes. As the glass cools further, it slowly becomes inflexible, but without bonding the crystals. This is why it can shatter or break so easily when knocked. However, glass never loses any of its original clarity, density or weight, making it an excellent medium for encapsulating and preserving artistic expression.

Lead glass (or crystal, as it is now more commonly known) has a brilliant finish and is the basic material of cut glass and most of the fine antique paperweights made. During the 1670s, the English glass-maker Ravenscroft perfected the manufacture of lead glass, taking the basic combination of silica and an alkali, and adding up to fifty per cent lead oxide to give the glass strength and a brilliant sheen. By the beginning of the nineteenth century, lead glass was being used extensively in France.

The making of a paperweight is the same today as it was in the mid-nineteenth century. It is an intricate process which requires accuracy and deliberation.

Small pots of different coloured glass are used to make the canes of millefiori (glass rods cut crosswise to reveal the minute designs). A hollow rod-shaped tool called a gathering iron is rolled over the molten glass, sticking the glass to the tip of the iron. The glass is then rolled into a cylinder over a slab of polished iron called a marver. The soft molten glass is next plunged into a pot containing glass of a different colour. The soft, coloured glass sticks to the cylindrical core, surrounding it evenly. This molten glass is again rolled over the marver to form the previous cylindrical shape and the process is repeated a third time.

Usually the soft mass is shaped to a star or hexagon by being dropped into a shallow pastry-type mould. A second iron, pontil or rod is then attached to the other end of the cylinder of glass and is held by two workers who stretch the glass as much as possible so that it becomes a thin and very fine rod. When this rod is less than a millimetre thick it is dropped into a wooden trough and left to cool. A number of rods are then heated up and combined to make millefiori canes.

Stages in making a Baccarat rooster silhouette cane
*Shown (**left**) are the mould, the silhouette and canes before and after stretching.*

A St Louis corncockle, 1845–60
*The five blue petals are edged and backed in white, and surround a stamen of yellow, pink and black canes (**below**).*
Diameter: 2½in (6.3cm)

This process is repeated in order to produce hundreds of canes in different colours and shapes, some of them containing tiny silhouettes: camels, deer, horses, griffins, goats, butterflies, elephants and dancing figures all feature as silhouettes in antique paperweights from the two great factories of Baccarat and St Louis. The third factory, Clichy, did not make silhouette canes.

Such accurate and precise silhouette designs require certain minor alterations to be made. First, an open iron mould is carved on the inside to the required shape of the silhouette. The mould is then heated and the dark coloured soft glass dropped into it. When the glass is adequately set but still hot the mould is opened and the motif removed by being attached to the rod and then coated with a layer of usually opaque, but sometimes coloured, glass. Finally, the glass is reheated and stretched into a long cane. The silhouette retains its shape perfectly and appears as a tiny dark figure against the bright light background. Often one finds several silhouettes strategically placed in a paperweight among hundreds of tiny, coloured millefiori canes.

When the canes are cold they are arranged according to the design and style of the paperweight. A thick flat ring with a handle is used to position the different coloured short canes in the middle of an iron mould and thereby form the pattern.

Inevitably, blank spaces occur and these are filled with canes of colourless or opaque and tinted glass. It is important to note, however, that each individual weight contains a large number of singularly designed canes. Once the canes have been arranged in the mould they are reheated to softening point so that they bind together.

The designs of non-millefiori paperweights—such as flowers, fruit, butterflies and reptiles—are made by hand. In the nineteenth century, many of these lampwork designs were made by workers at home, after they had finished their day's work at the factory. A piece of coloured glass is held with tweezers in front of a blowlamp and shaped as required. When all of the individual components have been made, they are assembled in an iron mould and heated up so that they join together.

In all paperweights, the method of forming the clear glass dome is the same. Using a rod dipped in clear molten glass, the millefiori or blown glass design is taken out of the mould. The rod, with the design now attached, is dipped into the molten glass to build up and form the crystal dome above the pattern. In order to achieve a smooth and uniform finish, the molten glass is shaped using a curved wooden mould. With the dome now in place, tongs are used to snap the paperweight away from the rod attached to its base, although you can often see where the rod has been; this is known as the pontil mark.

Finally, the paperweight is left in a cooling kiln (sometimes called an annealing oven) to toughen. The kiln allows plenty of time for the weight to cool at its own pace and thus prevents the glass from splintering or rupturing. The temperature in the kiln itself is slowly reduced over a period of twelve hours, or even longer if the paperweight is magnum size.

MILLEFIORI DESIGNS

The main components of millefiori paper-weights are colourful canes made up from bundles of glass rods heated up and bound together. Often, some of the individual rods are heated up and dropped into a mould to form a more elaborate cross-sectional design or a silhouette as the centre to a cane. These designs include the star, arrowhead, shamrock, honeycomb and cross.

When the glass-makers have made enough canes, they are cut into tiny pieces and arranged in a mould according to a formal pattern. The illustrations here show some of the most common millefiori weights. The most representative millefiori design is the close-pack (1), in which the canes are packed tightly together underneath the clear glass dome. In spaced millefiori weights (2) the canes are set apart at intervals, usually in rows or circles. Similarly, canes are set apart at regular intervals in chequered weights (3), but in this design the individual canes are separated by white or coloured latticinio twists. Concentric millefiori weights (4) are comprised of a central cane or group of canes, around which are organized a series of concentric circles made up of millefiori. Sometimes the millefiori canes make a chain or chains to form loops that often intertwine—these weights (5) are called garlands. In mushroom weights (6), a mushroom-shaped group of canes is encased in glass; the head of the mushroom is arranged as a group of close-pack or concentric millefiori, and the mushroom is usually surrounded by a twisting torsade.

*2 A Baccarat spaced millefiori, signed and dated 'B 1849' A variety of canes (**above**) placed at intervals above a bed of lace. Diameter: 2³⁄₈in (6cm)*

*1 A Baccarat close-pack, signed and dated 'B 1848' The archetypal paperweight design (**left**), with millefiori canes tightly encased beneath the clear glass dome. Diameter: 3in (7.6cm)*

3 *A Clichy chequer, 1845–60*
Twists of pink latticinio separate the canes.
Diameter: 3¹/₄in (8.2cm)

4 *A Clichy concentric, 1845–60*
Seven concentric circles set about a central cane.
Diameter: 3¹/₄in (8.2cm)

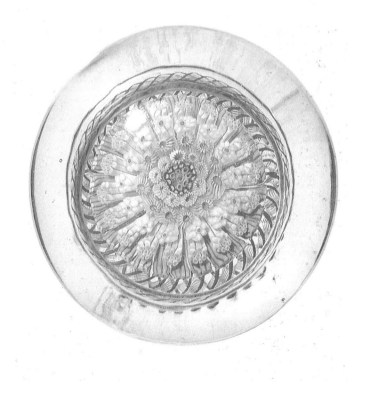

5 *A Clichy garland, 1845–60*
A garland of canes set above a dazzling blue ground.
Diameter: 3¹/₄in (8.2cm)

6 *A St Louis mushroom, 1845–60*
The head of the mushroom is a concentric design.
Diameter: 3in (7.6cm)

LAMPWORK DESIGNS

Many of the most charming paperweights feature designs made up of pieces of coloured glass shaped using a blowlamp to represent flowers, fruits or animals. The variety of these weights is enormous, and you will see many fine examples illustrated throughout the book. Shown here is a selection of flower and fruit weights, including some lampwork flowers before being encased in a paperweight. These two flowers and the paperweight below them (1) were made by Nicholas Lutz, who was trained at the Cristalleries de St Louis. Lutz worked at a number of glass factories in Europe before emigrating to America in 1860. The examples shown here were made around 1870–5, while Lutz was working at Sandwich.

As with all paperweights, however, the majority of the finest examples were made in France between 1845 and 1860. The most common lampwork designs feature flowers. The camomile, or pompom, is quite rare, but it is revealing to see two examples from different factories together (2): the St Louis weight (top) has much more feathery, delicate petals than the equivalent Baccarat weight (below), while the central millefiori canes are also quite different, and helpful in

establishing the factory of manufacture. The Baccarat bouquet (3) contains five camomiles, and the dramatic construction is enhanced by the printies cut into the glass dome. The Clichy edelweiss (4) seems quite crude in comparison to the camomiles, although the factory made some wonderful floral weights. Here, however, the precision and quality of the swirling latticinio almost calls attention to the rather rough-finished petals of the flower.

Fruits and vegetables also inspired paperweight designs, although they appear far less frequently. This strawberry weight (5) made by Baccarat shows a ripe strawberry growing on a stem that also includes an unripe fruit. The relative simplicity of the composition benefits from the generously radiating star-cut base. The weight is somewhat put to shame, however, by the glory of the Clichy wild strawberries (6). If the edelweiss is a somewhat lacklustre example of a Clichy flower weight, then this weight showcases the factory's magnificent qualities of colour and composition. The detail and delicacy of the stems and fruit and the pleasing symmetry of the design are among the finest work ever to have been encased in a glass paperweight.

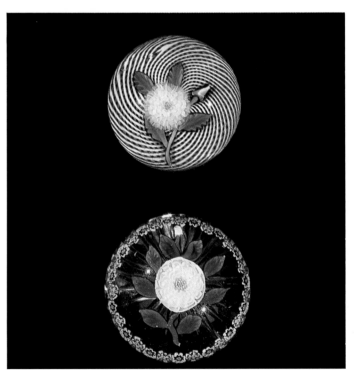

1 Lampwork flowers made by Nicholas Lutz while he was working at Sandwich, 1870–5
Diameter of weight: 2⅛in (5.4cm)

2 A St Louis camomile above swirling latticinio and a Baccarat camomile above a star-cut base, 1845–60
Diameters: 2⅞in (7.3cm); 3⅛in (7.9cm)

*3 A Baccarat bouquet containing five camomiles, faceted
with six side printies and a top printy, 1845–60
Diameter: 3⅝in (9.1cm)*

*4 A Clichy edelweiss and bud placed above a swirling
white latticinio ground, 1845–60
Diameter: 2⅞in (7.3cm)*

*5 Baccarat strawberries, one ripe and one unripe, are
seen growing from a leaved stem, 1845–60
Diameter: 3in (7.6cm)*

6 Clichy wild strawberries, les fraises des bois, *growing
on either side of a white flower, 1845–60
Diameter: 3in (7.6cm)*

NINETEENTH-CENTURY FRENCH PAPERWEIGHTS

GLASS PAPERWEIGHTS MADE IN FRANCE BETWEEN 1845 AND 1860 SET THE STANDARD BY WHICH ALL OTHERS ARE JUDGED. AMAZINGLY, PAPERWEIGHT-MAKING REACHED ITS PEAK OF SOPHISTICATION WITHIN A FEW YEARS OF THE MANUFACTURE OF THE FIRST PAPERWEIGHT. ALTHOUGH THE FRENCH GLASS INDUSTRY WAS GENERALLY IMITATIVE RATHER THAN INNOVATIVE, THE LAMPWORK DESIGNS —FLOWERS, BOUQUETS, BUTTERFLIES, REPTILES, FRUIT AND VEGETABLES— WERE A FRENCH INVENTION OF THE TIME.

BACCARAT

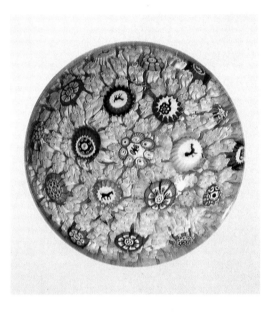

*A Baccarat carpet ground, signed and
dated 'B 1848'
Diameter: 3⅛in (7.9cm)*

*BACCARAT PRODUCED A WIDE
RANGE OF SUBJECTS, BUT IS
ESPECIALLY FAMOUS FOR ITS
SILHOUETTE CANES AND BEAUTIFUL
PANSIES. THE FACTORY SIGNED AND
DATED MANY OF ITS PAPERWEIGHTS.*

The Baccarat factory is situated between the Vosges mountains and the Black Forest near Luneville, Nancy. It was founded in Alsace-Lorraine, an area much fought over for many years by France and Germany. It has been under French rule since 1918, although from 1870–1918 it was a part of Germany.

The Sainte Anne glassworks were founded in Baccarat in 1764. Initially they produced industrial glass for utilitarian purposes, such as panes of glass and bottles. However, the glassworks were not a great success, and by 1814 only about 60 workers were employed in the factory and it was only just managing to pay their salaries.

In 1816, however, the Sainte Anne glassworks were bought by a Parisian, Aime-Gabriel d'Artigues, who had once been manager of the St Louis glassworks in Alsace. D'Artigues had already built up an enviable reputation for success, transforming the Voneche glassworks in Belgium—which he bought in 1802—into one of the major glass exporters to the rest of Europe. D'Artigues significantly improved the quality of the Voneche factory's output by introducing Ravenscroft's invention of lead crystal, and he would come to adopt the same tactic with Sainte Anne.

However, Napoleon's abdication in 1814 and his subsequent exile to Elba meant that France was experiencing great political and economic upheaval, and conditions in the glassworks in France at this time were particularly unsettled. Territories were being sub-divided and parts of France newly found themselves a part of the Netherlands. Domestic unrest in turn made it difficult for French glassworks to compete in the export market, and Britain, no longer affected by the continental blockade, fully exploited the chance to acquire new trading partners. In an attempt to combat this new threat, d'Artigues negotiated a deal in 1816 with King Louis XVIII: d'Artigues guaranteed to open a glassworks in France producing some 10,000 hundredweight of crystal per year if in turn he was allowed to import 6,000 hundredweight of rough crystal free of duty to France, for the following two years. By reducing the cost of raw materials, d'Artigues was able to manufacture glass more cheaply than foreign competitors and so assist the survival of both the Voneche and Sainte Anne glassworks.

On 15 May 1816 d'Artigues bought the Sainte Anne glassworks for 173lb (86.7kg) of fine gold, and by 9 April 1817 he could proudly boast of a Royal Warrant allowing him to open his new glassworks, the Verrerie

A Baccarat magnum bouquet, 1845–60
This is a superb bouquet, with pansies, a dahlia and a
camomile. It is faceted with six printies around the side
and another on top. The base is star-cut.
Diameter: 3³/₄in (9.5cm)

de Voneche à Baccarat. Being an enterprising man, d'Artigues also set up a separate factory for the production of lead oxide to facilitate the use of lead crystal, which soon became a trade mark of Baccarat glass. He also encouraged the workers to educate their children and the factory offered benefits such as sickness, redundancy and retirement aid.

Sadly, the Verrerie de Voneche à Baccarat could not afford the spending necessary to build up and maintain the workshops. D'Artigues also suffered ill health, and on 7 January 1823 he was forced to sell the company. In 1824 Voneche Baccarat became a limited company and by 1843 Voneche was dropped from the name; henceforward the glassworks were known simply as Baccarat.

Baccarat was one of the leading French paperweight makers, producing weights copiously and to a very high standard. The factory was also a major producer of mirrors, chandeliers and tableware. From the 1820s, Baccarat and St Louis were among the foremost producers of coloured glass and also the best: the repro-

duction and clarity of colour was quite splendid, and the two factories were unrivalled until 1839 when the Clichy factory began glass production, joining Baccarat and St Louis in their precision and colour.

In 1846 Baccarat was producing paperweights using various designs for decoration, but particularly mille-fiori. Baccarat competed at a number of exhibitions and won many medals for its high standards and marvellous designs. However, like the St Louis glassworks, Baccarat failed to exhibit at the Great Exhibition of 1851 at London's Crystal Palace, perhaps fearful of the competition. Given the enormous success and popularity of the Exhibition, the factory must have paid for its absence both in terms of custom and prestige; it learnt from its mistake, however, and from then on exhibited at all future exhibitions and fairs.

About half of Baccarat weights are signed and dated. The signature and date will always be found set in canes to one side of the weight, never in the centre, and the 'B' is usually set above the date. The letter and figures appear in blue, green or red, usually on a white cane. The 'B' is always attributed to Baccarat, since designers were forbidden from applying their own signatures to their work. Sometimes, and especially in the past, the 'B' has been mistaken for Bristol or Birmingham as well as for Bigaglia, the man responsible for reintroducing the art of latticinio and aventurine. The signature has also been attributed to the Battestinis of Venice, a family of paperweight-makers who left Italy for France and who changed their name to Bastet; however, it has never been established that they signed any of their weights and it is almost certain that any weight signed with a 'B' originates from the factory at Baccarat.

Sometimes Baccarat weights can be found with a date but no signature. A good example is the millefiori paperweight set in the cornerstone of the St Remy church at Baccarat. It is dated 1853, the year that the stone was laid. Although the church was destroyed during World War Two, it was rebuilt in 1953, and the millefiori in the cornerstone still remains. The paperweight was created by a man called Martin Kayser, a well-known master craftsman who began working at the Baccarat factory in 1827 when he was only thirteen years old.

In many respects the three main factories produced weights of remarkable similarity, and often it can be extremely difficult to tell them apart. However, there are some significant differences that can help one to identify a Baccarat from a St Louis and a Clichy. For example, the colour contrasts in a Baccarat weight tend to be much stronger, with hard blues and reds rather than the gentler pinks and pale blues used by the other two factories.

Certain canes and motifs, too, are particularly characteristic of Baccarat, such as the simplified versions of arrowheads, butterflies, honeycomb, trefoil, quatrefoil, shamrock and whorl. The star is as one

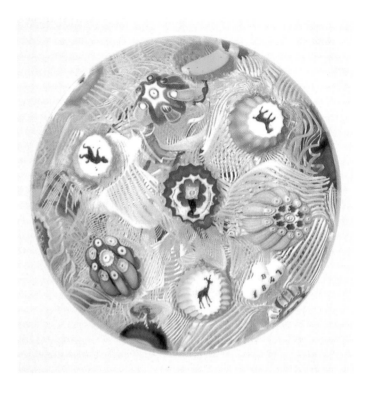

A Baccarat spaced millefiori, signed and dated 'B 1847' The millefiori sit on a bed of lace and are encased in clear glass. Silhouette canes are easily seen in designs like this. Diameter: 2¼in (5.7cm)

A Baccarat carpet ground, signed and dated 'B 1848' Set among the orange carpet ground canes are two concentric circles of larger canes, including a number of silhouettes. Diameter: 3⅛in (7.9cm)

imagines a star to be, but with additional points between the main five points. The arrowhead is just like an arrow pointing upwards, the butterfly is quite a simple butterfly and the honeycomb resembles a cross-section of honeycomb with large drops of honey between the combs. The trefoil and quatrefoil are simplified plants with, respectively, three or four leaves. The shamrock is similar to the trefoil and quatrefoil but also has a stem and can be found as a separate cane in special pattern weights. The whorl resembles an open-ended spiral.

Silhouettes, although not unique to Baccarat, are also a common feature. However, they are also of great significance to the St Louis factory as well as to Bacchus, a British glassworks founded in the nineteenth century in Birmingham. The Baccarat silhouettes include the dancing devil, and various animals such as the crane, deer, dog, dove, elephant, goat, horse, kangaroo, monkey, pheasant, rooster, stork (or pelican) and swan.

Emile Gridel, the nephew of the nineteenth-century industrialist and manager of the Baccarat factory, Jean-Baptiste Toussaint, had perhaps the greatest influence on the use of silhouette canes. Gridel had a passion for animals and later on in his life he became quite an expert on animal life and studied in great depth their behavioural activities. He was also a keen painter of animals. However, in 1846, at the age of only eight, he was making accurate and charming cut-outs of animals, which his uncle saw,

recognizing the potential use the silhouettes could be put to in the manufacture of paperweights. These original cut-outs were kept and treasured by Emile Gridel's family and still remain in their possession.

The most usual designs in Baccarat are, as mentioned before, millefiori. The most desirable, and collectable, examples are also signed and dated, and it is not as rare as one might imagine to find such a paperweight, although often one has to look very hard to find hidden in a cane a tiny B and, in another cane below it, a date. Usually, the date is 1847 or 1848, but other dated weights do exist, making the object rarer and more valuable if it is in good condition. Honeycomb canes are very typical of Baccarat and are a helpful way of trying to identify millefiori weights. Spaced millefiori weights are also quite common, with the millefiori canes usually scattered evenly over a bed of lace. Some of the canes might also contain tiny dancing silhouettes, making the signed and dated canes, which lie on a basket of latticinio, easier to identify. Close-pack millefioris come in sizes from 2–4in (5–10cm) and dates can be found in each size. Most have dates between 1846 and 1849, but one can acquire other dates such as 1853 and 1858. Rare dates often increase the value of a weight.

All millefiori canes are very tightly packed, with some silhouettes appearing intermittently. The canes fill most of the glass. Filigree twists are compressed between the canes on the inside so that no light shows through from the base of the weight.

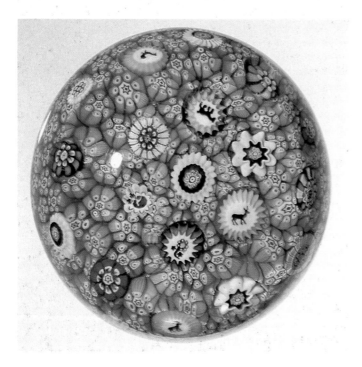

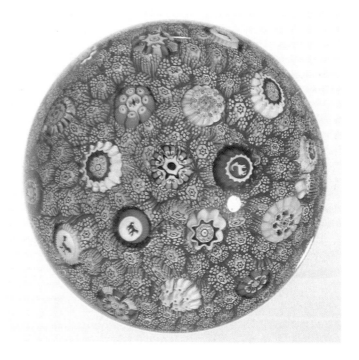

A Baccarat carpet ground, signed and dated 'B 1848'
A fine red carpet ground set with coloured canes. Five of the canes contain silhouettes: a goat, a deer, a bird, a horse and a rooster.
Diameter: 3in (7.6cm)

A Baccarat carpet ground, signed and dated 'B 1848'
This weight is set with colourful canes, including some silhouettes. The cane bearing the signature and the date can be seen on the far left-hand edge.
Diameter: 3in (7.6cm)

A Baccarat flat bouquet, 1845–60
*Three flowers are set in a triangular formation (**right**). The three blue and white cogwheel petals make the pansy unusual. Beneath the pansy are a red and white primrose and a white double clematis with an arrowhead centre. The base is star-cut.*
Diameter: 3in (7.6cm)

A Baccarat flat bouquet, 1845–60
*This is a very rare example (**above**), comprising a purple and yellow pansy, a red and white primrose with rounded petals, and a white wheatflower with blue spots.*
Diameter: 2³⁄₄in (7cm)

Two Baccarat canes: a trefoil and a stardust.

A Baccarat mushroom, 1845–60
*The mushroom inside this paperweight (**left**) has a 'head' formed by close-pack millefiori, in colours which are rather unusual for this factory. One of the canes is a silhouette. Around the mushroom is a red and white torsade.*
Diameter: 3in (7.6cm)

A Baccarat magnum bouquet, 1845–60
*A fine paperweight (**right**), in which the bouquet comprises a pansy, dahlia, rose and stylized flower, interspersed with green leaves to give a luxurious and beautiful contrast of colours. The star-cut base and oval printies further enhance the design.*
Diameter: 2⁷/8in (7.3cm)

Two Baccarat canes: a whorl and a flower silhouette

A Baccarat flat bouquet, 1845–60
*A magnificent arrangement (**left**) of three flowers including a blue and white primrose and two stylized flowers, one with blue and white arrowhead cogwheel petals, the other with red and white cogwheel petals and a dark blue bud.*
Diameter: 3in (7.6cm)

A Baccarat stylized flower, 1845–60
From the central pink and white cane radiate petals that
are blue, white, and then blue again. Around the stem and
the flower are eleven green leaves.
Diameter: 2⅞in (7.3cm)

A Baccarat wheatflower, 1845–60
This is a handsome example: the yellow wheatflower, here
with a bud and stem, is among the more unusual Baccarat
flower weights. The base is star-cut.
Diameter: 3in (7.6cm)

Alternatively one can find the millefiori canes scattered; this is known as spaced millefiori. Sometimes the canes are just on their own or else they sit on a bed of lace, the spirals of lace running in an anti-clockwise direction. The range of sizes for spaced millefiori weights is the same as for close-pack weights, and dated examples exist from 1847 to 1849, usually with a 'B' for Baccarat. Silhouettes are also in evidence and look particularly distinctive in spaced millefiori on lace because the pastry moulds are so exacting and precise. Spaced millefiori weights can also be enhanced by faceting.

Flowers can also be found, true to form and identifiable for those who know the species or their names. There are a number of different designs among Baccarat flower weights. Bouquets, which appear either flat or upright, are usually found in clear glass. The flat bouquets lie two-thirds of the way down or even nearer to the base of the glass. The upright bouquets are three-dimensional, and are sometimes found with a torsade of either blue, pink or red; in

both cases the bouquets have leaves. Sometimes the weights are faceted all over and sometimes printies are cut into the glass: these are similar techniques but produce highly different results.

Flowers are a prolific feature. They are found with a bud, usually with leaves, but less often with a stem, depending on how large the bloom is. The most popular flowers are the pansy, clematis, wheatflower, dahlia and primrose. Others are the poinsettia, rose, camomile, bluebell, buttercup and wallflower. All of these flowers can be found on their own or arranged as a bouquet with stylized flowers. They can be flat or upright. Sometimes there is a garland of florets around the edge and often the base is star-cut, either radiating generously right to the edge of the glass or just cut in the middle of the base. Colours are vivid and these weights are particularly attractive.

The flat pansy is one of the most typical of Baccarat paperweights. Whereas St Louis and Clichy produced relatively few pansy weights, Baccarat produced them prolifically and in a range of sizes. Good examples can be acquired for a price of £3–400 (U.S. $495–660), making Baccarat pansy weights an ideal starting point for someone wanting to build up a collection of antique weights. Usually the pansy is either purple, or deep red and yellow with variations. Sometimes it appears as a single flower, at other times with a bud. Most often the flower is set in clear glass, and more often than not with a star-cut base. It is made in miniature form as well as in the normal dimension of 2–2½in (5–6.3cm). It is easily identifiable and differences may be observed between Baccarat pansies and their St Louis and Clichy equivalents, both of which are more delicate in colour and form. There are also differences between early and late Baccarat pansies.

The carpet ground, perhaps one of the most successful Baccarat designs, appears in varying forms: the overall carpet, the carpet of clusters and the stardust carpet ground. The carpet and carpet of clusters look rather like closely packed garlands. The chequer resembles a chequerboard of large silhouettes integrated with other canes. All of these weights are extremely rare.

Colour grounds are also very rare. Translucent grounds of blue, red and green appear and are associated with the garland design. Jasper grounds were also made during the nineteenth century.

Concentrics are usually found in clear glass with the canes formed on a curve. Silhouettes appear in certain canes, the colour combination of the canes being restrained. Faceting can also be a feature. Some of these concentrics rest on lace and are similar to those made by Clichy. A helpful guide to distinguishing between the two is that the Baccarat gauze twists are formed anti-clockwise and the pastry mould canes are more clearly defined.

Fruits such as strawberries, pears, apples, cherries, peaches and apricots are realistically depicted. The pear is the most common of all of them and its design is particularly life-like. The apples, peaches and cherries are scarce, but as with all of the fruits they are of the highest quality. Last but not least the apricots must be the rarest of them all, with fruits so deliciously composed that one wants to eat them.

The garland (a chain formation of intertwining canes) is a very popular design used by Baccarat. Mostly, the garland is set in clear glass but it can occasionally be found in coloured glass, or set on lace. This formation can also be seen on carpet grounds. Garland weights look particularly interesting through printies and can also be found with a double overlay.

The mushroom weight looks very much as the fungus, hence its name. Most examples of the mushroom appear with a realistically coloured stem leading to a domed top of close-pack millefiori, the long canes reaching to the top of the glass where they are crisply cut away. Around the edge of the stem of the mushroom there is often a twisted torsade in either blue or red, leading in an anti-clockwise direction. When the

A Baccarat carpet ground, 1845–60
*The ground (**above**) is comprised of stardust canes. There are also a central concentric cluster and six silhouettes: a monkey, goat, rooster, dog, horse and deer.*
Diameter: 3⅛ (7.9cm)

A Baccarat dog rose, 1845–60
*This is a very good example of a dog rose (**right**). In addition to the flower itself, there are a bud, nine green leaves and a stem, and the whole design is enhanced by the surrounding ring of florets and the bed of white lace.*
Diameter: 2¾in (7cm)

mushroom appears inside a double overlay the twisted torsade is usually omitted. Double overlays, however, are somewhat unusual. The rarest mushroom is the white stardust, one of which can be seen at the Sturbridge Village Museum, Massachusetts. Mushroom weights can also be faceted in miniature size and may be found in the form of a pedestal, with the mushroom placed above a basket of filigree. The mushroom weight can also have silhouettes and there is record of a Baccarat mushroom with Clichy roses.

Overlays occur in rich red, green or blue, and double overlays in varying shades of blue and pink. The weights are cut with printies and often, towards the bottom edge of the glass, fluting. Some of the overlays have gilded attractive decoration applied to them, painted in a typical style with small pretty floral patterns. The interior decoration is usually a garland

*Four Baccarat silhouette canes (**left to right**): a rooster, pelican, horse and goat.*

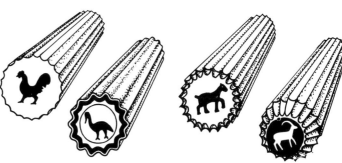

*A Baccarat convolvulus,
1845–60*
*The vermillion flower
(**left**) grows from a curved
green stalk on which there
are also a bud and, near
the base, two green leaves.
The convolvulus is
perhaps the rarest of the
Baccarat flower weights.
This example is set in clear
glass with a star-cut base.
Diameter: 2½in (6.3cm)*

*A Baccarat pear weight,
1845–60*
*The orange and yellow
pears (**above**) hang from a
stem with six green leaves.
The base is star-cut.
Diameter: 2½in (6.3cm)*

*A Baccarat camomile,
1845–60*
*An interesting camomile
(**above**) with blue leaves
fringed with white, and a
white bud. A garland of
florets decorate the
perimeter.
Diameter: 2⅞in (7.3cm)*

*A Baccarat primrose,
1845–60*
*The yellow primrose and
white bud (**above**) grow
from a stem with five green
leaves. The flower is
surrounded by a garland
of blue and white, and
pink and white, florets and
the base is star-cut.
Diameter: 2⅝in (6.7cm)*

*A Baccarat clematis,
1845–60*
*The red clematis (**above**) is
complemented by a bud,
leaves and a stem.
Diameter: 2⅝in (6.7cm)*

*A Baccarat dog silhouette
cane.*

or garlands, or a mushroom either with a close-pack
or a concentric design. The interior colouring tends
to be rather soft and mollifying, with a star-cut base
typical of Baccarat.

The pedestal is not a design that was made in
abundance. The canes are formed in a concentric way,
the actual pedestal with latticinio and blue, pink, red
and white twisted ribbons. These are usually about
2½–3in (6.3–7.6cm) in diameter, but magnum
weights can also be found.

The butterfly is quite common among Baccarat
weights, appearing as a design on its own or hovering
over a flower. When it appears with a flower, the
butterfly usually obscures about one-third of the bloom
and leaves. The butterflies are usually multi-coloured
and are among the most successful, attractive and

A Baccarat 'ducks on a pond', 1845–60
Diameter: 3¹/8in (7.9cm)
Value: £6,000 (London, 1986)

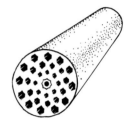

A Baccarat honeycomb cane.

A Baccarat butterfly and clematis, 1845–60
*The multi-coloured butterfly (**left**) has aquamarine eyes and hovers above about one-third of the white clematis.*
Diameter: 2¹/2in (6.3cm)

collectable of Baccarat designs.

The rock weight rates as the most uninteresting. In itself it is really rather empty, although it often forms the base to snake and lizard weights. The rock is greeny brown in colour with creamy speckles. Sizes range from miniature through to magnum. When Baccarat snakes and lizards do not appear on rock grounds they rest on muslin. The snakes are usually a reddy black colour or brown on dappled green. As with torsades, air bubbles are a feature, supporting the theory that it was impossible to achieve either of these designs without the bubbles. Sometimes these weights are faceted resembling the type of cutting on a diamond known as a brilliant cut. They are quite rare and, like all lampwork designs, undated.

The lizard poses a problem, being difficult to attri-

bute with certainty to the factory of origin. Lizard weights were made by Baccarat, St Louis and the little-known factory of Pantin, the so-called fourth factory.

The scrambled weight appears in varying qualities, and it is sometimes hard to distinguish all of the original canes. A helpful way to identify the Baccarat scramble is that the twisted filigrees are set at right angles to one another, which is not the case with St Louis or Clichy scrambles. Baccarat scrambles are surprisingly rare; although only occasionally dated, they can be found throughout the size range.

Finally, and most controversially, weights containing ducks on a pond have been dubiously ascribed to Baccarat. They are very rare and show two or three small ducks swimming on green algae, in clear glass with printies and a star-cut base.

ST LOUIS

ST LOUIS WAS THE FIRST FRENCH FACTORY TO MAKE A DATED PAPER-WEIGHT. ITS MAGNIFICENT AND DISTINCTIVE CROWN WEIGHTS TYPIFY THE FACTORY'S BOLD USE OF COLOUR AND FORM.

A St Louis crown, 1845–60
A striking combination of yellow, white and black twists radiating from a central cluster. Diameter: 3⅛in (7.9cm)

The original glassworks on the site now occupied by the Verreries de Saint Louis were established in 1586. However, the Thirty Years War (1618–48) forced the Munzthal glassworks to close down, and it was not until 1767 that the St Louis glassworks were opened. Almost immediately, in 1768, they were bought by François de Lasalle Aine & Cie, who ran the glassworks until 1809 when the company was sold to Messrs Seiler and Walter.

In 1829, Seiler & Walter made the company into a limited shareholding company trading under the name of Compagnie des Verreries et Cristalleries de Saint Louis. In 1831, a retail shop owned by the company opened in Paris selling glass not only from St Louis but also from Baccarat. The glassware sold was quite utilitarian initially, athough decorative glass, including paperweights, soon became a part of the stock, and by 1855 the St Louis factory was producing imitation agate, marble and malachite.

At the Paris Expositions in 1834, 1839, 1844 and 1867, St Louis glass was evident and highly sought after. However, like Baccarat, the factory failed to exhibit at the Great Exhibition of 1851 in London.

Despite the high standards and popularity of St Louis glass throughout the second half of the nineteenth century, the work of the factory exhibited at the Exposition in 1867 was obviously not particularly remarkable, since little comment is made about it in reports at the time. There is absolutely no reference to St Louis work being exhibited at the 1878 Paris Exposition, even though the other two French factories of Baccarat and Clichy did attend, along with the fourth factory, Pantin.

As with Baccarat, the glassworks were situated in the Vosges Mountains. In 1870, French defeat in the Franco-Prussian War resulted in seizure of most of Alsace-Lorraine by Prussia (soon itself to become a part of Germany), and it was not until the end of World War I in 1918 that the area, which included the St Louis glassworks, was formally returned to France. During the 1920s, St Louis reaffirmed its links with designs of French influence, such as enamelled glass. Designers including Dufrene and Goupy were commissioned by St Louis and the factory also appointed a number of designers from La Maitrise design department of the Galleries Lafayette store in Paris.

The first dated St Louis paperweight was made in 1845, making it the first of the three famous factories to produce a dated specimen. However, the quality of

A St Louis carpet ground, signed and dated 'SL 1848'
The blue and white carpet weight **(right)** includes six silhouette canes: one in the centre, and the others regularly spaced around it.
Diameter: 2¹/₂in (6.3cm)

A St Louis silhouette cane of two dancing figures.

A St Louis mushroom, signed and dated 'SL 1848'
From the central Catherine Wheel cane radiate five concentric circles of canes **(above far right)**. Surrounding the mushroom is a blue and white torsade.
Diameter:2³/₄in (7cm)

Two St Louis canes: a devil silhouette and a hollow tube.

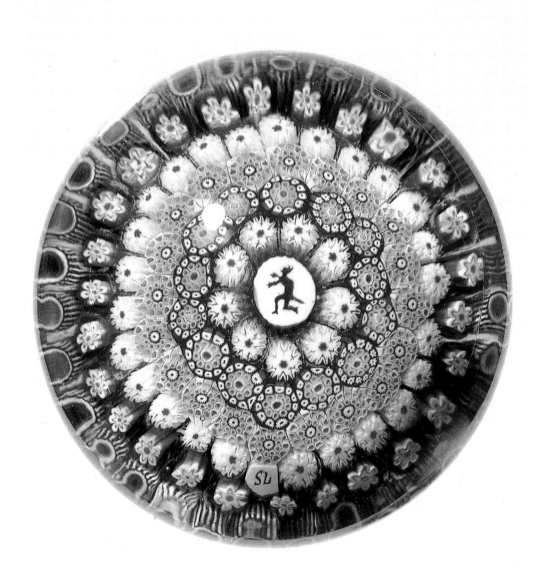

A St Louis concentric, 1845–60
The canes forming the concentric circles **(right)** are mainly blue, red and white. The central cane contains a devil silhouette.
Diameter: 3in (7.6cm)

this weight means that one can be sure that other paperweights were made prior to this date. Besides paperweight production, St Louis also increased its output of wonderful glass objects such as decanters, inkwells and rulers.

St Louis soon began enlarging their range and perfecting their designs. Although in many respects St Louis weights are very similar to those of Baccarat, they are distinguished by the St Louis trademarks of clarity and subtlety of colour.

The shape of St Louis weights is variable. The glass has a great deal more clarity and less striations than is found in Baccarat weights. Although the use of star-cutting to the base of the paperweight does appear it

is, again, less frequent a feature than in Baccarat weights, and is confined to certain upright bouquets, mushrooms and flowers. Most of the designs are placed quite close to the base of the weight, although latticinio baskets are an exception, occurring about half way up the dome.

1847 and 1848 are the most usual dates found on weights from the St Louis factory, but some are also dated from 1845 to 1849. Sometimes the signature of 'S L' appears above the date. The date is coloured, and can be blue, mauve, red or dark purple, with the signature appearing in black or blue. Occasionally the signature is found on its own. St Louis signed and dated far fewer of its (millefiori) paperweights than

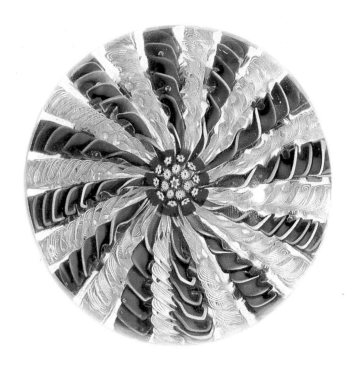

A St Louis panelled carpet ground, 1845–60
*This design (**above**) is very rare. The close-pack ground is divided into panels by fine twisted ribbons.*
Diameter: 3in (7.6cm)

A St Louis crown, 1845–60
*An attractive crown (**above far right**) of blue and yellow, and red and green, twisted ribbons alternating between twisted opaque white latticinio.*
Diameter: 2½in (6.3cm)

A St Louis magnum crown, 1845–60
*This is an important, rare and magnificent weight (**left**), with red, white and blue twists. The central cane is yellow, blue and white.*
Diameter: 4in (10.1cm)

A St Louis crown, 1845–60
*A magnificent weight (**right**) of green, white, red and yellow twisted ribbons and white latticinio.*
Diameter: 3⅛in (7.9cm)

Baccarat, despite being the first French factory to make a dated paperweight. Concentrics, centred silhouetted cane weights and mushrooms are the three most likely designs to bear the signature and date. Scrambles periodically appear with a date as do some of the related objects, such as scent bottles. Concentrics sometimes just bear the initials 'SL'.

The variety of canes is more limited than those of the Baccarat and Clichy factories. St Louis tended to specialize more in flowers, fruits, vegetables and snakes. The basic colouring of the St Louis weights tends towards the subtle greens, blues and pinks, or to the very definite reds, harder greens, blues and yellows. Many weights have a combination of the softer and more positive colours. White is used frequently in intertwining ribbon twists, latticinio, lace and muslin. The crown weight is perhaps the most distinctive of all the St Louis designs. These weights are hollow and the decoration is of coloured twisted ribbons running through and around white opaque latticinio. The ribbons and latticinio fill the whole of the glass, following the shape of the dome. In the centre at the top is a cluster of tiny millefiori canes or a single, larger cane. Usually the ribbons are of two contrasting colours, such as blue and red, yellow and blue or green and red. Sometimes three or four colours are used and recently a five-colour combination was discovered: blue and white, blue and yellow, red and green, red and blue and salmon pink and white. This was obviously an exciting and special commission, although no records of its manufacture or sale exist to provide further information.

Sometimes the crown of ribbons and latticinio does not completely fill the glass, but this is not a significant factor in assessing the quality and value. What is important is to note whether the whole crown is well centred and does not slant too much to one side. Crowns can be found from miniature to 3¾in (9.5cm). The crown weight was never produced with faceting.

Approximately 30 per cent of St Louis paperweights are flower weights, some true to form and others stylized, some of them flat and others upright bouquets. However, the factory is most renowned for its prolific output of fine, individual flowers, including the clematis, pansy, camomile, anemone, dahlia and fuchsia.

The dahlia is perhaps the most popular of all the flowers used by the factory. St Louis dahlias are very splendid and extremely pleasing to the eye. They are usually blue, a red, purple or mauve. The rarest examples are yellow with tiny black markings. The centre of the bloom is very small in comparison to the other flower weights. Green leaves can be seen jutting out from the vast blooms which fill the glass. These weights are very impressive. The blooms should be well centred and the bases are often star-cut.

The clematis is also a fairly popular flower, seen either as a single flower or as a double. Most of them rest on a latticinio ground, but the rarest have blue or pink jasper grounds or rest on aventurine. The clematis are either gentian blue or pink, with yellow or orange, or occasionally white, centres, a yellow or white stamen and usually four emerald green serrated leaves. Occasionally there is also a bud, but this can be

A St Louis clematis,
1845–60
*The blue, striped petals of this flower (**right**) radiate from a central yellow stamen.*
Diameter: 2⅞in (7.3cm)

Two St Louis canes: a horse silhouette and a star.

A St Louis camomile,
1845–60
*This many-petalled white flower above a swirling latticinio ground in tomato red (**below**) is very rare.*
Diameter: 3in (7.6cm)

difficult to recognize, being tightly closed and little more than an extension to the bloom. The petals are usually striped in subtle shades of blue, purple and pink, or pink and white.

Camomile or pompoms are perhaps the third most popular of the St Louis flower weights. Swirls of white thin latticinio on a red or pink translucent ground are used to form the background to the white frilly petalled bloom, and sometimes a bud is included. The thin white swirls of latticinio are set in a clockwise direction, providing a useful point of distinction from Baccarat weights, where the latticinio swirls anti-clockwise. Their size is usually about 2½in (6.3cm) in diameter. The design sits low down in the glass and although the base of the design is translucent any glass above the pompom is clear. The rarest examples do not contain white latticinio but rather a swirl in rich tomato red.

Fuchsias are usually red with blue, the lesser quality ones being paler. The flower heads are suspended from a narrow and fragile orangey brown stem with leaves, the blooms and buds profuse and intermingled. St Louis fuchsias are set in clear glass against a latticinio trellis ground, and range in size from 2½– 3¾in (6.3–9.5cm) in diameter.

Unlike the Baccarat factory, which produced the pansy in profusion, the St Louis pansy is quite a rare specimen, seen on its own, with a stylized flower or as a pair of pansies set side by side. The base of the weight is diamond cut all over and the flower is set in clear glass resting on a latticinio or a jasper ground. The St Louis pansy is much simpler in design than the Baccarat pansy. Sizes range from about 2½– 3½in (6.3–8.9cm).

The primrose is also another rare flower used by St Louis. Usually it consists of a blue bloom with a golden stamen and pale green leaves, set against a white latticinio trellis. Such weights are extremely difficult to acquire.

The convolvulus is probably the rarest St Louis flower paperweight. The flower is pale pink, with white petals in the middle, and the stem, which is leaved, is a vibrant emerald green. The convolvulus is usually found resting on white latticinio trellising.

Bouquets are either flat or upright. Although flower weights are plentiful they are not seen as often appearing as flat bouquets. These weights are very attractive and are somewhat more delicate than the Baccarat flat bouquets. An intricate pattern is formed by the intertwining leaves and flowers. The colours used are soft, true to the St Louis theme, yet the intermittent use of the rich blue colouring of the pelargonium makes a charming contrast. Sometimes stems are seen and sometimes just flowerheads and leaves. Again, the green of the leaves and stem is a softer shade than is found in Baccarat weights. These flowers are realistically expressed in St Louis's fine glass interpretation, with the bouquets set in the middle of the clear glass.

A St Louis flat bouquet, 1845–60
This is an unusual flat bouquet, combining two flowers, one blue and one white, with two multi-coloured canes. The flowers and canes rest on a flourish of green leaves. Diameter: 2½in (6.3cm)

A St Louis fuchsia, 1845–60
The flower and two buds are growing on an orange stem on which there are also four veined green leaves. The design rests on an opaque white swirling latticinio ground. Diameter: 2in (5cm)

A St Louis upright bouquet, 1845–60
The bouquet consists of a blue flower with white buds and
a single pink bud. It is interspersed with green leaves and
surrounded by a blue and white torsade.
Diameter: 2½in (6.3cm)

A St Louis magnum upright bouquet, 1845–60
This is a rare type of weight. The upright posy consists of
numerous tiny, colourful flowers surrounded by rich green
leaves.
Diameter: 4in (10.1cm)

The flat bouquets were usually made using three or four canes to make up a posy of idealized or true flowers, the bouquets also including leaves with serrated edges. These flat bouquets appear in clear and coloured glass and may also be faceted or fluted. Fine examples of this type of weight can be acquired, from the artfully simple to the intricately complex. Sizes are from miniature to 3in (7.6cm).

The upright bouquet is three-dimensional and fairly rare. It is often found with cutting around the glass and usually a torsade. However, in the magnum size some upright bouquets stand on their own in clear glass with diamond faceting. These particular weights are extremely rare in magnum size. The colours of the bouquets are rich and distinctive and include foliage as well as flower blooms and buds. From every angle the intensity of the bouquet can be seen.

The upright bouquets of standard size are as impressive. Although easier to find than the magnums, they are still not that common. They appear mainly in blues, with torsades of blue, red, yellow, green or coral. The base of the weights, as with the flat bouquets, often has strawberry cutting. The bouquet is situated in the centre of the glass but the flowers do not project widely.

The fruits and vegetables of the St Louis factory are grouped in latticinio baskets or set in clear glass on their own. The vegetable weights are rarer than

the fruits, and both types are characterized by the use of strong colours. Strawberries, cherries, pears and grapes are the fruits used; turnips, carrots and radishes, the vegetables. Usually a weight either contains fruit or vegetables, but they can be found mixed together. Sometimes the glass is cut with diamond faceting or with varying sizes of concave windows ('printies') which create interesting perspectives.

The St Louis fruit paperweights are typically 2½–3½in (6.3–8.9cm) in diameter. Some of the fruits appear on their own, such as cherries, apples, grapes and pears but often there is a variety. Occasionally, the blossom of the fruit is included, resting on latticinio and set in clear glass. The cherries are bright red, the apples a pinky colour with yellow stripes, the grapes a very deep purple, and the pears are green, yellow or red. Plums are bright blue and the oranges and lemons are the appropriate colouring; all three of these fruits are rare finds. Rarer still are black grapes and strawberries, the latter seen growing on a green stalk with yellowy green leaves and surmounted by a white flower with a solid yellow stamen. The strawberries rest above a ground of swirling latticinio threads, as do most of the St Louis fruit weights, although some are simply set in clear glass.

The vegetables are, if anything, even rarer: they tend to be grouped together with six or seven turnips, for example, set in a basket of latticinio. The turnips

A St Louis cherry,
1845–60
This pretty miniature
paperweight (above)
depicts two cherries
suspended from a yellow
stalk with three green
leaves.
Diameter: 2in (5cm)

A St Louis strawberry,
1845–60
This weight (above)
comprises two red
strawberries with a white
flower between them.
There is a stem with four
green leaves. The fruit
rests on a white double
swirling latticinio ground.
Diameter: 3in (7.6cm)

A St Louis fruit weight,
1845–60
Three cherries, two
oranges and a lemon are
interspersed between green
leaves (left). The fruit and
leaves rest on a swirling
opaque white latticinio
ground.
Diameter: 2¹/₂in (6.3cm)

Two St Louis canes: an
arrowhead and a dog
silhouette.

A St Louis cross, 1845–60
Examples of millefiori cross weights are rare. This one
***(above)** consists of a central cluster of canes from which*
radiate four bands of white stardust canes.
Diameter: 2³/4in (7cm)

A St Louis diamond-shaped millefiori, 1845–60
*This is an extremely unusual design **(right)**. The canes*
are set in six diamond-shaped groups on a white latticinio
ground.
Diameter: 3in (7.6cm)

are mauve, purple, white or yellow and the vegetables
do have stalks. Sometimes the turnips are red and
white and may be interpreted as radishes. The sizes of
these weights are similar to the fruit weights.

Millefiori weights from St Louis appear in varying
forms, one of the rarest being the millefiori cross
weight. This is extremely attractive and takes the
form of a white and salmon pink cluster from which
radiate four bands of white stardust canes flanked by

A St Louis carpet ground concentric, 1845–60
This is an important paperweight. The central cluster is
surrounded by ribbed, tubular canes in a pattern of white,

blue, brick-red and white again.
Diameter: 3¼in (8.2cm)
Value: £6,500 (London, 1986)

a twisted blue and amber mass of close millefiori canes in white, amber, blue, pistachio green and white including a flower silhouette. These weights are 2½–3½in (6.3–8.9cm) in diameter.

Other millefioris which are more typical of St Louis are the concentrics. These weights often include silhouettes. If there is only one, the silhouette is placed in the centre and the concentric millefioris circle it; if a number of silhouettes appear, however, then they tend to be placed symmetrically throughout the design. The silhouettes used in St Louis concentrics are the dog, turkey, dancing devil, stylized flower and camel. The most usual colour of silhouettes in a concentric weight is blue on white, but they also come in greens, pinks and reds of varying shades. These concentrics fill the glass, which is always clear, and are very pleasing to the eye. The size of canes used varies according to the size of the paperweight.

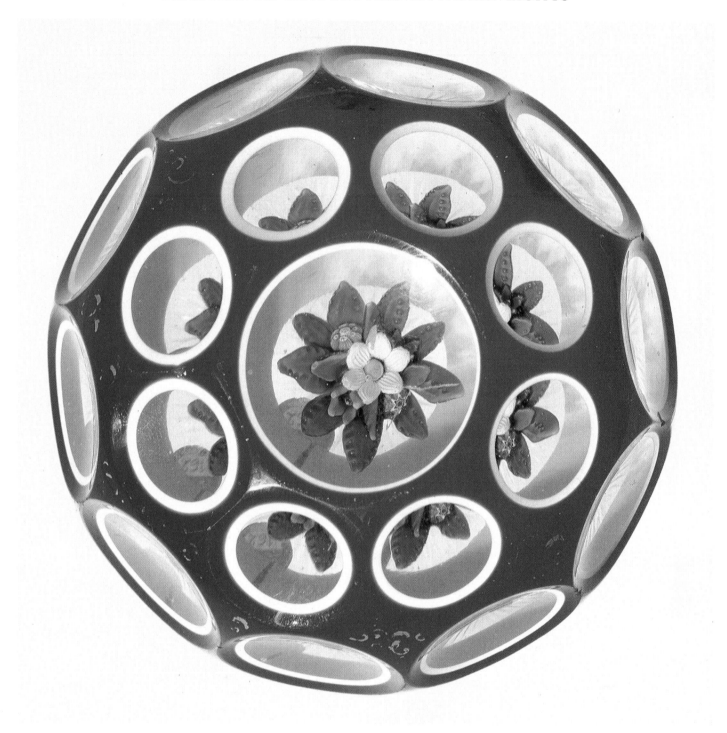

Concentric mushroom millefioris are also fairly usual. These are similar to the Baccarat mushrooms, and it is seldom easy to distinguish between the two. A useful guide is to look at the torsade: if the bands run clockwise over the tape (which is visible through the thin twisting strand) then it is a St Louis. Also, the dome or tuft of the mushroom, is usually set as a concentric whereas Baccarat are mainly close-packs. The colours used are blue, white, pistachio green or pink. These weights are usually about 2½ to 3½in (6.3–8.9cm) in diameter and are set in clear glass, often with a star-cut base. The torsades are either loosely twisted or tightly bound around the tape.

Sometimes a pedestal can be found attached to the

A St Louis double overlay upright bouquet, 1845–60
This fine bouquet is encased in a blue double overlay. The glass is cut with nineteen printies.
Diameter: 3in (7.6cm)
Value: £13,000 (London, 1986)

base of the millefiori weight. This is excessively rare. The foot itself has white latticinio trellising.

The St Louis overlays are really quite spectacular. They are highly sought after and magnificent, a valuable, rare and very exciting addition to any collection. Sometimes gilding is applied to the coloured overlay which often encases an upright bouquet with green

A St Louis snake, 1845–60
The green snake has the red eyes and nose typical of St
Louis snakes. The reptile rests on a bed of lace. The glass
is heavily faceted.
Diameter: 2¼in (5.7cm)

leaves. The flowers usually represent real specimens and are either blue, pink or white. The central bloom is either an entirely white flower or one with deep blue petals and a yellow stamen. Alternatively, the internal design may be a millefiori floral bouquet comprising blue, yellow, white, pink or red clusters of canes in an accumulation of fours, fives or sixes.

The colours of the overlays are dark blue, green or pink and very occasionally opaque white. Six concave printies are cut around the sides, with a larger printy on the top. All St Louis overlays have a star-cut base. They are not found in miniature form and are usually about 2½–3½in (6.3–8.9cm) in diameter.

Snakes are also typical of the St Louis factory. The reptile rests curled on a bed of white latticinio or on a coloured ground, and is set in clear glass with the sides occasionally faceted. The snakes have red eyes and are usually either pink with green mottled marking or speckled green in colour. Again, these weights are not found in miniature form and are usually 2½–3in (6.3–7.6cm) in diameter.

CLICHY

CLICHY HAD A BRIEF BUT BRILLIANT HISTORY, RIVALLING THE OUTPUT OF ITS WELL-ESTABLISHED RIVALS, BACCARAT AND ST LOUIS, ONLY A FEW SHORT YEARS AFTER ITS FOUNDATION.

A Clichy bouquet, 1845–60
A rare blue pansy flanked by a Clichy rose.
The base is star-cut.
Diameter: 2¾in (7cm)

Clichy should not be underestimated in any way for its lack of a long history. Weights produced by the factory during the classic period are no less sophisticated than those of Baccarat and St Louis, and are perhaps the most endearing. There is some doubt about the precise date of the founding of the Clichy factory. One theory is that it was founded at Sèvres in about 1838 by Rouyer and Maës and then moved to the Paris suburb of Clichy prior to the Paris Exhibition of 1844. Another idea is that it was founded at Billancourt (Pont-de-Sèvres) in 1837 and moved swiftly to Clichy in 1839. It seems that the latter is the more likely, since the work of M. Maës of Clichy-la-Garenne was catalogued by the magazine *Les Beaux Arts* as having been exhibited at the 1839 Paris Exhibition held in the Champs Elysées. By 1844, Clichy was well established, and at the Paris Exhibition that year the factory showed a selection of its work to highlight the marvellous standards already achieved.

The high standards and output meant that this factory was a major competitor of Baccarat and St Louis. By 1849, Clichy dominated the market for glass paperweights and was unable to meet the demand for its product. This caused alarm among the other factories,

and Baccarat and St Louis were constantly aware of the standards they had to achieve in order to remain in competition. By this time, Clichy was manufacturing weights from a special kind of glass which was soda-based and was known as boracic glass. This type of glass was used in the Clichy exhibits at the long-running and vast Exhibition of 1849 in the Champs Elysées in Paris. Much attention was paid to the results obtained using boracic glass, which produced a wonderful effect of clarity, making the internal design appear sharper. Ravenscroft's invention of lead crystal had previously been thought to produce the best, and clearest, glass, but Clichy's boracic glass equalled lead crystal in quality. Additionally, boracic glass produced a wonderful clarity and did not suffer with age from a form of yellowing associated with an excess of lead in crystal. This is not to say that the Baccarat and St Louis glass became yellower over the years, but it is interesting to note that boracic glass could be used as successfully as lead crystal.

Clichy was the only factory out of the three to exhibit at the Great Exhibition of 1851 in London, possibly because Baccarat and St Louis were not confident that their work would match that of their newly-founded rival. The jewel among the collection of Clichy weights

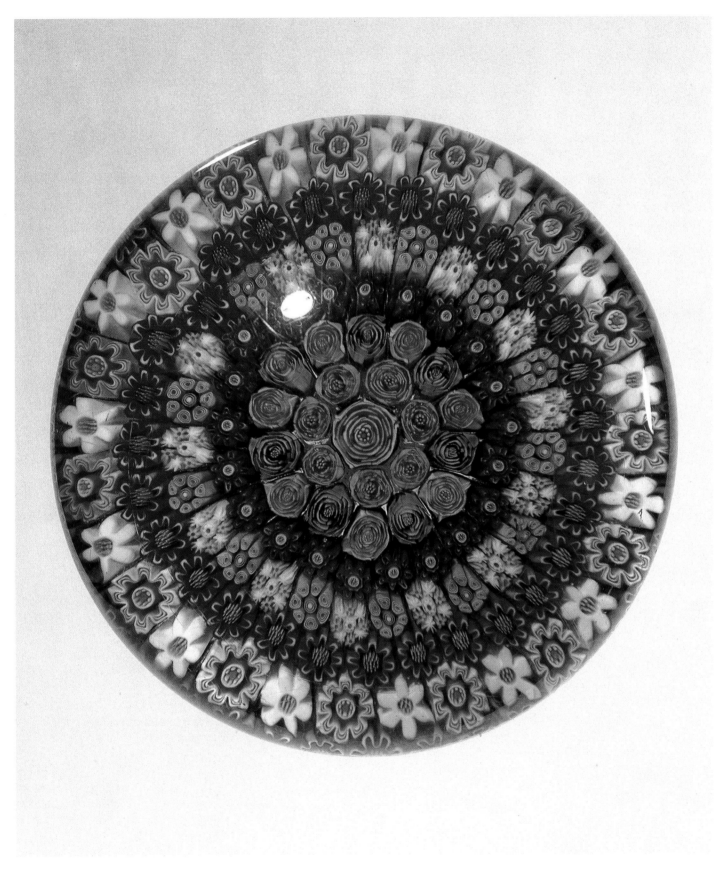

A Clichy magnum concentric, 1845–60
Around the central Clichy rose cane are two circles of
blue, pink and green rose canes, and five additional
circles of canes in blue, pink, green, red, white and yellow.
Diameter: 4¼in (10.8cm)

A group of Clichy flower weights, 1845–60
Most Clichy flower weights are stylized. Shown here are a blue flower on a moss ground (**right**), _a stylized group of four flowers on a single stem_ (**far right**), _a stylized flower with blue and white striped petals and a bud_ (**below, far right**), _and a bouquet including a pansy and Clichy rose and thistle canes_ (**below right**).

A group of Clichy flower weights, 1845–60
Most Clichy flower weights are stylized. Shown here are a blue flower on a moss ground (**right**), _a stylized group of four flowers on a single stem_ (**far right**), _a stylized flower with blue and white striped petals and a bud_ (**below, far right**), _and a bouquet including a pansy and Clichy rose and thistle canes_ (**below right**).

A Clichy hollow tube cane.

on show was an exceptional commission: a millefiori weight which had engraved on the base the monogram 'V.A.', with a crown above and the inscription 'Londres, 1851' beneath. This is unique and was clearly intended for Queen Victoria and Prince Albert. The weight is 3¾in (9.5cm) in diameter and is in a fitted leather case. It is the only Clichy weight with engraving to the base, and the date also makes it unique. Clichy weights occasionally appear with an initial 'C', or 'CL' in one cane and 'ICHY' in another, or 'CLICHY' written in full, but their weights are never dated.

Clichy showed some fine paperweights at the 1851 Great Exhibition earning the factory a special prize, chiefly in recognition of the fine use of overlays appearing in many colours such as blue, black, green, yellow, white, pink, gold and red.

In 1853, Clichy was once again represented at the great New York Fair in the Crystal Palace on Fifth Avenue at 42nd Street. It was obvious that under the direction of M. Maës the Clichy factory was thriving, and once again the work was well received and appreciated at the Fair. Besides paperweights, other glass articles were made which typify Victorian demands such as scent bottles, vases, door plates, vinaigrettes and door knobs.

By 1885, however, Clichy was no longer producing paperweights, and the factory was taken over by Sèvres, the famous porcelain factory run by the Landier family. The factory was renamed Cristalleries de Sèvres et Clichy, but by now the influences of M. Maës and M. Clemandot were only memories. The factory's subsequent output bore no resemblance to anything produced during the classic period, and unlike Baccarat and St Louis, Clichy never again produced paperweights. It is amazing to think that after its highly successful formative years from 1839 (or, less likely, 1844) such an invigorating company should so abruptly cease to produce fine objects. In 1867, M.

*A Clichy concentric,
1845–60
This is a charming
miniature millefiori
paperweight, and includes
a circle of nine pink Clichy
rose canes encircling the
central cane. The
concentric circles rise up to
the central cane, and
viewed from above appear
to fill the whole of the
glass.
Diameter: 1³⁄₄in (4.4cm)*

A Clichy rose cane.

Maës exhibited at the Paris exhibition, but this time the work was in fine flint glass; no paperweights are mentioned in connection with this date, Exhibition or gentleman. It is likely that this is when the decline of Clichy began. The years of unqualified success were over, the export market to countries such as Japan was stagnating, and Clichy could no longer count itself among the foremost glass producers as it had been during the '40s, '50s and early '60s.

The typical Clichy weight is slightly lighter and generally of a more delicate design than the equivalent Baccarat and St Louis weights. Clichy weights are extremely charming and endearing to look at, in subtle, passive colours. The most significant feature of Clichy weights is the cabbage rose cane, which is usually pink but is also found in blue or green. The rose resembles a cabbage rose found in Provence in the south of France that is used for making rosewater. Surrounding the rose is a pale green perimeter depicted in the

same manner as the flower head, but intended as an addition to represent the leaves. The Clichy rose appears in an occasional Baccarat paperweight, although this is exceedingly rare. Sometimes, the rose appears as a single flower growing from a green stem and set in clear glass (see page 7).

Although the Clichy rose is frequently used and is perhaps the most typical characteristic found in weights produced by the factory, it is by no means a trademark. Flowers, and especially roses, were so much a part of decoration during the Victorian era that it is only to be expected they should occur to such a great extent in paperweights produced at the time, not only by Clichy, but also Baccarat, St Louis and the other paperweight factories. The rose had been widely used in heraldry, for example, and for 500 years the Houses of York and Lancaster in the north of England had used the white and the red roses respectively as their insignia. The rose has always been a frequent motif

A Clichy garland, 1845–60
The central cane is surrounded by three circles. These are
set within a pink cinquefoil garland.
Diameter: 2³/₄in (7cm)
Value: £3,500 (London, 1985)

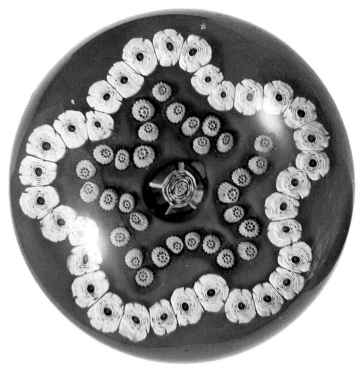

A Clichy garland, 1845–60
Above the blue ground are a central Clichy rose cane and
two cinquefoil garlands.
Diameter: 3¹/₈in (7.9cm)
Value: £1,200 (London, 1985)

used in textiles, porcelain, paintings, robes, coins, glass, jewellery and stone fountains, as well as in paperweights. Sometimes these roses are a purely decorative feature and at other times they convey a meaning. With paperweights there is no particular connotation attached to the rose except its charm and beauty.

Bouquets are not always easy to find. The most unusual bouquets are those that are tied at the bottom of the stem with a pink or, very rarely, a blue ribbon. The untied bouquets, although unusual, are easier to find than the tied bouquets. The pansy is a common feature in the Clichy bouquet and can be seen with a Clichy rose in its larger form. Some of the other flowers are stylized; others include the dahlia and clematis in colours of blue, striped pink, mauve, violet, white and lilac. Buds, stems and foliage are also included in the bouquets. These bouquets are set against a latticinio ground or just in clear glass. It has also been known for a bouquet to be set on a dark green moss ground, but this type of weight is extremely rare. Bouquets range in size from 2½–3½in (6.3–8.9cm) in diameter.

Millefiori represent a high proportion of Clichy paperweights. The Clichy rose appears regularly, but by no means always, in the pattern. The pink rose is the most used but blue, white and green roses also appear in a circular cluster. These weights are much rarer. The millefiori Clichy weight tends to adopt much more of a formal pattern, with a colour dominat-

ing the theme. Pinks are commonest, but blues or greens predominate in some examples. The canes are often encased in a striped basket of cobalt blue and white, green and white, or pink and white. The Clichy millefiori usually forms a pattern in a more structured way, such as a concentric or clusters of canes divided into a pattern by latticinio twists. Sometimes the millefiori canes form a ring around a cluster of central florets, a formation of canes taking the shape of a horseshoe, a close-pack or a spaced millefiori. All of these appear on grounds of tomato red, translucent red, cobalt blue, dark blue, green or in clear glass.

The Clichy factory was particularly adept at choosing colour combinations. Through their definite selection and contrast of colours, Clichy weights perhaps rate as the finest of the three factories in their effect. The colours are very varied: different shades of blue, green, pink, purple, red and yellow can be seen, ranging from bright, very clear colours to darker colours. The brighter colours tend to be sharper than those of the Baccarat and St Louis factories.

The mushroom design also features with the Clichy factory, and some of these are extremely rare. The millefiori domes of the mushrooms are formed in much the same way as the millefiori weights themselves. The main difference is that the internal design, although no less defined, is on a much smaller scale. Again, the mushroom millefiori forms a colour scheme, which even beneath the coloured overlay is very

CLICHY

A Clichy magnum
chequer, 1845–60
Short lengths of white
spiral cables separate three
concentric circles.
Diameter: 4³⁄₈in (11.1cm)

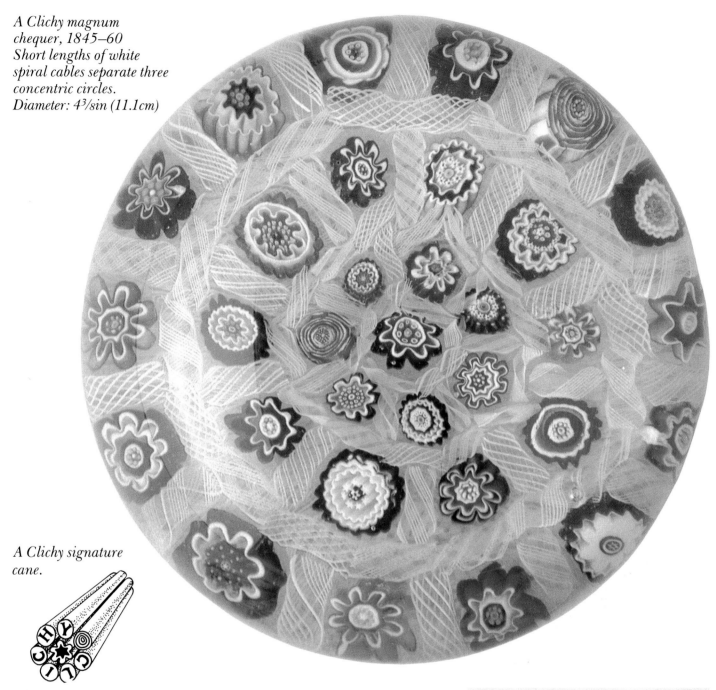

A Clichy signature
cane.

A Clichy spaced millefiori,
1845–60
This weight (right) is
particularly unusual
because the canes are set
on a dark blue ground.
Diameter: 2⁵⁄₈in (6.7cm)

A Clichy mushroom,
1845–60
The head of the mushroom
(far right) is a concentric.
The glass is cut with six
printies around the edge
and one on the top.
Diameter: 2³⁄₄in (7cm)

A group of Clichy overlays
These are very desirable weights. The white eggshell
*overlay (**top left**) is the only single overlay above a close-*
pack; the others are all double overlays encasing
concentric millefiori mushrooms.

evident and clear. Sometimes the stem of the mushroom takes the form of a striped encasement, similar
to the striped baskets encasing some of the millefiori
weights; the usual colours are pink and white, blue
and white, pale purple and white, or green and white.
The bases are often cut with strawberry diamond
cutting and the size is approximately 3in (7.6cm).

Even more collectable than Clichy mushrooms are
the overlays. Turquoise is the most usual colour for
single overlays, but tomato red, blue, moss green and
white are also applied to the glass. Double overlays—
which consist of a strong second colour on top of
opaque white, with the white forming a frame around

the printies—are even more sought after. All of the
overlay weights feature five printies cut into the sides
of the glass, with a further printy cut into the top.
Sometimes, but only very rarely, a sixth printy is cut
into the side of the glass. The base is usually cut with
strawberry-diamond cutting.

A Clichy swirl, 1845–60
Probably the design most associated with Clichy, this fine
swirl has twists of cobalt blue and white, with a Clichy rose
at the apex.
Diameter: 2¾in (7cm)

Swirls are another great characteristic of the Clichy factory. Although a significant number of them were made, almost all of them are marked by the central cane being off-centre. The canes take a variety of forms, usually a millefiori cluster, a pastry-mould cane, or—most covetable of all—the famous and enchanting Clichy rose. The colours used in the swirl are usually cobalt blue and white, purple and white, or green and white, although very rare Clichy swirls combine more than two colours, such as pink, green and white or purple, green and white. All range in size from approximately 2–3½in (5–8.9cm).

Scrambles also feature; they are more ordered than Baccarat and St Louis scrambles, and the colours tend to be brighter. Sizes range from 2–3in (5–7.6cm).

Miniature weights appear more often in the Clichy factory than in any other. Most of the miniatures are millefiori, either close-pack or spaced, but small posies are also to be found. Many of them include a Clichy

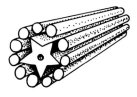

A Clichy pansy, 1845–60
Clichy pansies are rare weights. Here, two large purple
petals are set above three cream petals with white
markings and purple stripes. The flower rests on an
opaque white, swirling latticinio ground.
Diameter: 2⅞in (7.3cm)

A Clichy double clematis, 1845–60
The bloom is formed by two rows of pointed and ribbed
white petals with pink shading around the red and white
stardust stamen. The green stem bears a cluster of green
leaves and a single bud.
Diameter: 2½in (6.3cm)

A Clichy scramble, 1845–60
This is a good scramble, and includes four Clichy rose
canes. The colours are strong and bright.
Diameter: 3in (7.6cm)

Two Clichy canes (left): moss and a whorl.

rose. Swirls sometimes appear in miniature form.

Clichy also produced sulphides or incrustations, most frequently featuring portraits of Pope Pius IX, Queen Victoria and Napoleon. The last two are the most popularly collected, and prices for them are correspondingly higher. The sulphide busts are set against a ground of vivid blue, crimson or purple, which are all good colours to contrast the white of the sulphide. Sometimes a ring of florets appears, usually including Clichy roses.

The pedestal also features in much the same way as in Baccarat and St Louis. It is decorated with close-pack, concentric or chequered millefiori and the lengths of canes run vertically downwards. The base is decorated with latticinio or a circle of roses.

The single flowers used by the Clichy factory include the pansy, although it does not occur as frequently as in Baccarat or even St Louis paperweights. The upper petals appear in shades of blue, red and violet, the lower petals in varying degrees of pale and darker yellow. They are set in clear glass or on latticinio, and are extremely attractive.

The convolvulus (or Morning Glory) is the most charming and pleasurable flower to look at. It is very rare, and either lies on latticinio or is set in clear glass. The rarest examples are of a double convolvulus in combination with a stylized flower. There is always a stem and the leaves tend to be long, tapering off to a thin point at the end. The colouring of the flowerhead is pale and delicate with a band of pale blue, pink, purple and yellow around the top edge of the bloom. The base is usually star-cut, and the size is generally about 2½ (6.3cm) in diameter.

The clematis is also very pretty and fresh. It often occurs in an inspirational form, not entirely representative of the natural flower although there is a strong resemblance. Sometimes the petals are striped pale blue and white or pink, purple and rusty red. The central cane forming the stamen can be a variety of colours, such as yellow, green and pink, blue and white, or a darker shade of pink and white. The stem and leaves always look fresh, although their colour varies from pale through to dark green, depending on the colour of the petals.

Fruit weights are not typically associated with Clichy. There is considerable doubt as to whether they produced any fruit weights at all, but it is possible that strawberries were used very occasionally. In some respects it would be strange if none were included in the Clichy factory's output when Baccarat and St Louis were producing them so successfully at the time. Vegetable weights were not made by Clichy.

Unlike Baccarat and St Louis, Clichy no longer produces paperweights. The history of this enormously accomplished factory is sadly brief. By 1870, the factory's reputation was already in decline, and when, in 1885, Clichy was bought by Sèvres, paperweight production had ceased, never to be revived.

PANTIN

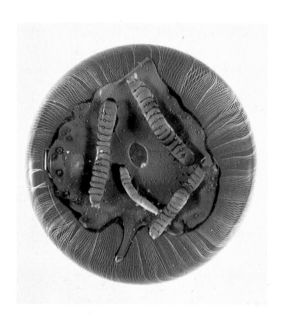

Pantin silkworms, c. 1880
This weight set a world record price of
$143,000 at Sotheby's, New York in 1983.

THOUGH PROBABLY OPERATING AFTER WHAT IS GENERALLY CONSIDERED AS THE CLASSIC PERIOD OF FRENCH PRODUCTION, PANTIN IS JUSTIFIABLY FAMOUS FOR ITS RARE AND STARTLING LAMPWORK DESIGNS.

Little is known about the output of this intriguing factory, which is usually referred to as Pantin but is also sometimes called the Fourth Factory. Pantin's association with glass-making does not stretch back in history as far as Baccarat, St Louis or indeed Clichy. The company experienced many changes in a relatively short space of time. However, the factory's reputation is considerable, and was consolidated when, in 1983, a Pantin paperweight was sold by Sotheby's in New York for the enormous sum of $143,000, the highest price ever paid for a paperweight. The weight is 3⅝in (9.2cm) in diameter, and depicts four mauve silkworms resting on a partially eaten mulberry leaf, set above radiating white latticinio strands above a blue opaque ground.

The factory was founded in 1850 and began trading under the name of Monot and Company, based at La Villette, a small area then just outside of Paris. A number of moves and an even greater number of changes in the company's name took place over the next fifty years, but finally, in about 1900, the Christallerie de Pantin was founded in a suburb of Paris, run by Sainte Hilaire, Touvier de Varreux et Compagnie.

Paperweight production precedes this date, however: in 1878, trading under the name of Monot, Père et Fils, et Stumpf, a number of three-dimensional (upright) paperweight designs had been produced. Designs featured lizards, snakes, squirrels and flowers, and a number of lizard and large flower weights have been attributed to Pantin, since the realistic detail seems most typical of this factory. Their provenance is generally far from certain, however. Air bubbles appear to be a deliberate feature of Pantin paperweights, although it may just be that the techniques and designs—in many ways so much more ambitious than those of the three main factories—were less refined. The bold interior forms of Pantin paperweights were perhaps inspired by the three-dimensional designs of the old-fashioned snow-storm paperweights.

Although Pantin did not produce a great number of paperweights it should be noted that the factory's low production does not in any way undermine the quality and originality of their weights, as the record price for the silk-worm weight proves.

A Pantin lizard, c. 1878
A coiled green lizard on a rock ground. Only eleven weights survive which were definitely made by Pantin.
Diameter: 4½in (11.4cm)

RELATED OBJECTS

The designs and techniques used in making paperweights were applied to so-called related objects. Made during the 1850s, these objects include scent bottles, inkwells, toilet sets – comprising bottles, mugs and a tray – decanters, vases, tazzas and shot glasses. Depending on the object, decoration was usually to the finials, stoppers and bases, and most often took the form of close-pack, spaced or scrambled millefiori. As we have seen, millefiori was being used in decorative glass made by the Romans in the second century, so it is not surprising that interest should be renewed during the classic period of paperweight production; what is perhaps most remarkable, indeed, is that related objects were not manufactured in greater quantity.

Decoration ranges from the simple to the elaborate, and the objects are as attractive as they are practical. Although only very few of the related objects are signed, each of the French factories produced distinctive wares. The Clichy factory, for instance, made coloured grounds decorated with garlands and Clichy roses. Baccarat was most prolific in the use of floral decoration and millefiori, and St Louis favoured the coloured twisted ribbons used in crown weights, and also opaque white, blue or pink latticinio.

Baccarat objects include vases with dispersed millefiori canes in clear glass and a pair of vases deeply cut with a scroll design, each with a pansy and rose bouquet. Tazzas were popular, usually with close-pack millefiori on the dish and base and opaque white latticinio twisting up the stem.

St Louis made a number of hand coolers, shaped in the form of an egg and often cut with printies. The internal designs vary from upright bouquets to close-pack millefiori and twisted filigree canes with twisted coloured ribbons. St Louis vases were most often made with a crown design in the base. Scent bottles, too, have bases and stoppers of crowns, as well as scrambled or close-pack millefiori, while the actual bottles are sometimes decorated with latticinio.

Clichy scent bottles are exquisite, the bottles and stoppers fluted and cut with printies, and the bases decorated with garlands, roses or millefiori canes. Clichy vases decorated with scrambled millefiori can be very attractive, and there is a lovely inkwell cut with printies and decorated with millefiori canes including Clichy roses.

As with the paperweights themselves, most of the related objects were made by the three great French factories. However, the Whitefriars factory in London made something of a speciality of related objects, including inkwells, decanters, glasses and doorstops. Bacchus, by contrast, made almost no related objects (certainly very few remain) and the same is generally true for the American factories, the exception being Sandwich: candlesticks, doorknobs and decanters all featured in the factory's production, and Nicholas Lutz made glass pens as gifts for his friends.

A Clichy water decanter,
1845–60
The decanter and
matching stopper are
decorated with gilt above
the green and white
filigree spiral. The spiral
extends from the base to the
rim, and the stopper is
surmounted by a cup-
shaped finial in a similar
pattern.
Height: 8½in (21.6cm)

Two Whitefriars inkwells,
c. 1848
Both of these inkwells are
decorated with concentric
millefiori canes in the base
and stopper. The larger
one contains canes in red,
white, blue and
aquamarine, while the
smaller (or 'lady's') inkwell
is decorated with canes of
blue, pink, green and
lavender, four of which
bear the date '1848'.
Heights: 5¾in (14.6cm)
and 4in (10.1cm)

NINETEENTH-CENTURY BRITISH PAPERWEIGHTS

RAVENSCROFT'S INVENTION OF LEAD GLASS IN THE 1670s SHOULD HAVE PLACED THE BRITISH GLASS INDUSTRY IN THE FOREFRONT OF EUROPEAN MANUFACTURERS. HOWEVER, IN 1745, CROMWELL'S GOVERNMENT LEVIED A TAX ON GLASS PRODUCTS. WHEN, IN 1845, THE GLASS EXCISE DUTY WAS FINALLY ABOLISHED, THE BRITISH GLASS INDUSTRY EXPERIENCED A PERIOD OF GROWTH. THE FINEST BRITISH PAPERWEIGHTS WERE MADE BY BACCHUS IN BIRMINGHAM AND WHITEFRIARS IN LONDON.

WHITEFRIARS

*A Whitefriars concentric, dated '1848'
Five rather poorly formed circles
surround a large central cane.
Diameter: 3¹⁄₄in (8.3cm)*

*WHILE MANUFACTURING MILLE-
FIORI PAPERWEIGHTS FROM ABOUT
1850 ONWARDS, THIS FACTORY IS
PERHAPS MORE FAMOUS FOR ITS
DEVELOPMENT OF RELATED
OBJECTS THAN FOR THE WEIGHTS
THEMSELVES.*

There is an interesting tale attached to the site of Whitefriars. Located in an area of London known as the City and running south from Fleet Street towards the River Thames, this site was for many years a monastery until it was destroyed in 1538. The disappearance of this monastery, however, did not lead to the site being deconsecrated, and the land remained a neutral ground where no one could be arrested, offering a safe retreat for the highwaymen and various tax- and debt-dodgers of the day.

In 1538 the White Friars Monastery was demolished, and it was not until 1680 that a new building was constructed for the purposes of making glass. The sacred ground on which the factory was built meant that no taxes could be collected, and it has been recorded that on one occasion several tax collectors visited the glass factory, only to be chased away by someone wielding a red-hot glass on the end of a blow-iron. Needless to say, the tax collectors did not pursue their task.

Some twenty years later, glass-making was an increasingly popular and profitable business in London, and by 1700 the capital could boast eleven factories that were manufacturing lead glass, White-friars included. Clear glass decanters were the vogue of the day in the early 1700s, and many were being produced. Drinking glasses were also popular and obviously complemented the demand for decanters. The most popular style was of a classic Baroque stem and bowl which first came to fashion in Britain in the 1670s. The bowls of the glasses were usually decorated with diamond-point cutting, or with shallow wheel-engraving (a decorative pattern applied by a rotating wheel which grinds the design or inscription into the surface of the glass).

By the nineteenth century, Whitefriars was producing many articles of glassware such as telescope glass, watch dials and stained-glass windows. White-friars was by this time under the ownership of James Powell and Sons. James Powell was himself a pioneer glass-maker: born in 1774, he lived and worked in Bristol as a glass-maker. In the late eighteenth century Bristol was a centre for the production of flint glass (which is lighter and less clear than crystal), and was also famous for the manufacture of opaque white glass. However, by 1800 Bristol was rapidly dwindling as a centre for glass production, and so in 1835 James Powell left for London where he bought a share of the Whitefriars Company. At the time of the Great

Exhibition in 1851, Whitefriars was in effect represented, although it was trading under the name of James Powell & Sons. It is very likely that examples of Whitefriars paperweights were included among the exhibits, although, as with all of the other paperweight-producing factories who showed at the Exhibition, no weights are actually catalogued.

Whitefriars began manufacturing paperweights in 1848. The factory did not produce a great number, however, and those that remain are all millefioris, and mainly take the form of related objects such as inkwells, scent bottles and decanters, rather than paperweights themselves.

Whitefriars weights appear in three different shapes: rather tall and broad with a ridge at the bottom; more conventionally shaped paperweights such as the ones produced by Baccarat, Clichy and St Louis; and very flat weights, with the bottom edge and the curve of the dome meeting at a 45-degree angle.

The colours of the Whitefriars paperweights can be strong and definite such as angry red, cold blue and a luscious pink, but contrasting this can be pale yellows and white. In fact, for every hard colour there is a corresponding and complementary soft one, so that the yellow, for example, does not always appear to be delicate but can also be more dense. The combination of these colours can be seen in the concentric designs. A large sitting white rabbit is a cane sometimes found in early Whitefriars paperweights. Although it is unusual, if you do find one then you can be sure that it is a Whitefriars paperweight dating from the classic period. The later weights include heart-, diamond- and club-shaped canes.

The close-pack millefiori weights are very traditional and are closely set. As in the French style, the canes are set low and are very colourful, although the colour routine is imaginatively played out to a less rigorous scheme than in the French weights.

The concentric weights are the most prolific, ranging in diameter from 2¼ to 4½in (5.7-11.4cm). Unlike the close-pack millefioris, and rather surprisingly, a number of Whitefriars concentric weights appear to be rather repetitive and uninteresting. However, this is not always the case, and some examples show that Whitefriars could produce extremely powerful concentric designs, such as one recorded with bright electric blue, scarlet and pink, and musty yellow concentrics. This is an extremely handsome weight, perfectly balanced and with a highly compatible colour scheme.

Some examples of chequered weights do exist, but Whitefriars was not successful at producing this design. The chequered weights that have survived are good examples of bad chequered weights, highlighting how difficult this technique is to achieve successfully. The twisted canes are all rather jumbled, leaving large gaps of unfilled surface design.

Perhaps most famous of all are the Whitefriars inkwells. There are two different styles, so similar, however, that they really amount to a variation on the same theme. The earlier design (dating from the late 1840s) is more bulbous than the second, more extended version. The stopper of the early type is taller and slimmer, while in the later type the stopper bears resemblance to an actual paperweight. Both inkwells are footed. Close-pack or concentric designs appear in both kinds of inkwell, usually at the base of the well and at the base of the stopper. Some of the early inkwells are also faceted.

Along with the inkwells, other related objects produced by Whitefriars include decanters and wine glasses, which had been a staple of Whitefriars glass production since the beginning of the nineteenth century. The canes are arranged in a simple fashion but not very carefully. Whitefriars also made doorstops— these were decorated with millefiori concentrics and proved a highly successful commission. One doorstop bears the date 1848.

Whitefriars continue to make paperweights, including ones to commemorate the coronation of Queen Elizabeth II in 1953; these are all concentric millefioris and are inscribed 'E II R, 1953'.

Dated Whitefriars paperweights survive for the years 1848 and 1953 only. The date in 1848 weights is made up from four individual canes, whereas in the 1953 weights, the whole date appears in one cane, in combination with the commemorative 'E II R'.

A pair of Whitefriars candlesticks, c. 1850
Filigree twists in the stems lead to concentrics in the bases.
The canes are predominantly yellow, blue and pink, and
the design is shallow in profile, a typical characteristic of
Whitefriars.

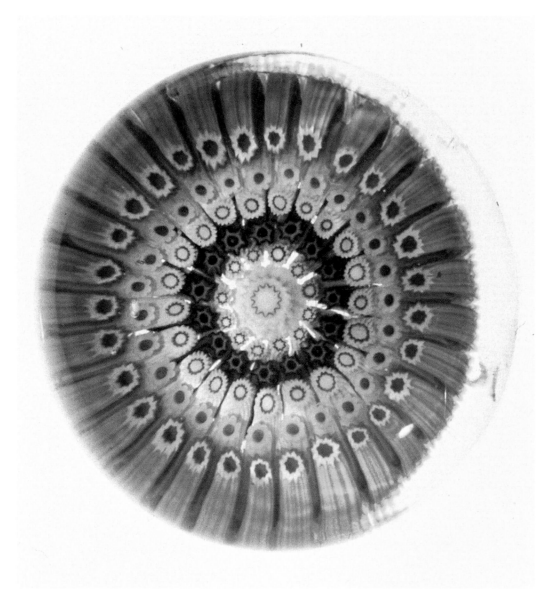

A magnum concentric, attributed to Whitefriars, c.1850
*The profile and colour of the canes suggest this is a Whitefriars paperweight (**left**). Four concentric circles surround the central white and pastry mould cane.*
Diameter: 4¹⁄₈in (10.5cm)

A Whitefriars commemorative, 1976
*This modern weight (**right**) commemorates the American bicentennial (1776–1976). It is faceted with five side printies and a large circular printy on top.*
Diameter: 3¹⁄₈in (7.9cm)

A Whitefriars inkwell, dated '1848'
*The clear glass bottle (**above**) encases concentrics in the base and stopper. The date appears crudely in four canes in one of the circles in the base.*
Height: 6in (15.3cm)

BACCHUS

ALTHOUGH USING ONLY A SMALL RANGE OF CANE COLOURS, BACCHUS TRANSFORMED THIS LIMITATION INTO A STYLISTIC VIRTUE, PRODUCING SOME OF THE FINEST MILLEFIORI WEIGHTS AVAILABLE.

A Bacchus mushroom, 1848–55
Four concentric circles form the head.
Glass is cut with flutes and printies.
Diameter: 3½in (8.9cm)

The Union Glass Works was first listed in 1818 situated in Dartmouth Street, Birmingham. It was owned by Bacchus, Green & Green, but in 1833 the company changed its name to George Bacchus & Co. In September 1840, George Bacchus died, and the following year the company's name was amended to George Bacchus & Sons and eventually, in 1858, to just Bacchus & Sons.

The Bacchus factory primarily made domestic glassware such as drinking glasses which were often engraved, cut or enamelled. They also produced decanters, jugs, vases and heavy, glass rolling pins. By 1848 the factory had begun to produce paperweights as a result of research into the art of Venetian glass-making, and at the Society of Arts in 1848 Bacchus exhibited very successfully a selection of their paperweights which were admired and, in Britain at least, deemed to be as fine as contemporary French and Bohemian weights.

In 1849, Bacchus exhibited at another exhibition in Birmingham, sponsored by the British Association. It was an interesting and historic moment as this was the opening exhibition at Bingley Hall, the first ever building in Britain to be established as a permanent site for exhibitions. The Exhibition of Manufactures and Art was a great success, attracting many hundreds of exhibitors and significant coverage in British newspapers. Among the Bacchus display of various cut, engraved, painted, enamelled and gilded glassware in the form of vases, jugs, candlesticks, goblets, bells and toilet bottles were a number of Bacchus paperweights. The Bacchus paperweights were, in fact, catalogued as 'letter weights', an early and short-lived term for paperweights before the translation of the French 'presse-papier' gained currency.

By 1851, at the time of the Great Exhibition in London, Bacchus showed some examples of their fine glassware, winning an award for the quality of their cut glass. Among the other Bacchus exhibits were no doubt some of their paperweights. However, the factory did not produce a large number of paperweights—probably only a few hundred in total—and it seems that for this reason it was not taken as seriously as, or

A Bacchus concentric, 1848–55
*A large ruffle cane in the middle (**right**), is surrounded by canes of blue, pale pink and white.*
Diameter: 3½in (8.9cm)

BACCHUS

*A Bacchus concentric,
1848–55
This predominantly pink
weight (right) has four
circles of canes around a
large central red and white
ruffle.
Diameter: 3½in (8.9cm)*

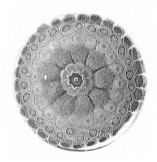

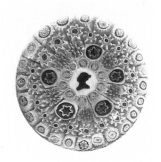

*A Bacchus concentric,
1848–55
The central silhouette of a
woman's profile (left) is
surrounded by four
concentric circles in blues
and pinks.
Diameter: 2⅞in (7.3cm)*

*Two Bacchus canes: a cog
and a crimp.*

A Bacchus concentric, 1848–55
This fine concentric **(right)** *in subtle shades of green, pink and lavender is typical of good Bacchus paperweights. Despite the subdued tones, the clever combination of canes effects a sophisticated design.*
Diameter: 3 ¹/₂in (8.9cm)

A Bacchus star cane.

seen as a threat to, the three main French factories.

Bacchus weights are heavier in weight and their average size is also greater, approximately 3–3½in (7.6–8.9cm) in diameter. The dome is flatter making the circumference wider and the internal design fuller, running right down to the base of the glass. The clarity of the glass is not as transparent as that of the three great French factories, and under a strong magnifying glass fragments of impurities are visible in Bacchus weights, despite the use of lead glass.

Four canes are typical of the Bacchus factory. The star cane resembles a six-pointed star, and was produced in a variety of colours with two dark outer circular rings. The ruffle consists of a cane enclosing a design of six or eight square-edged petals around two loosely-depicted, six-pointed stars, with a circle in the centre. The crimp is the simplest of the four: eight rounded petals encase a dark coloured ring and a lighter circle in the middle. The cog is comprised of three concentric circles, the second and third of which are divided by a zig-zag motif, lending the cane a cog-like appearance.

The colours and tones of the canes used by the Bacchus factory bear no resemblance to those used by the French factories. Bacchus tended towards more placid and cooler colours, suggesting that their canes were more important than their colours. Some of the canes look more like pieces of porcelain or plaster than glass. The colours of the canes range through opaque white, blue, pink, green, mauve and aquamarine. Despite the relatively narrow spectrum, Bacchus cleverly achieved subtle colour effects by placing certain colours adjacent to one another to give the impression of rich sophistication. These weights have much more of a texture and depth to them than would be expected.

There are no recorded dated Bacchus paperweights, suggesting that the factory never included, or even

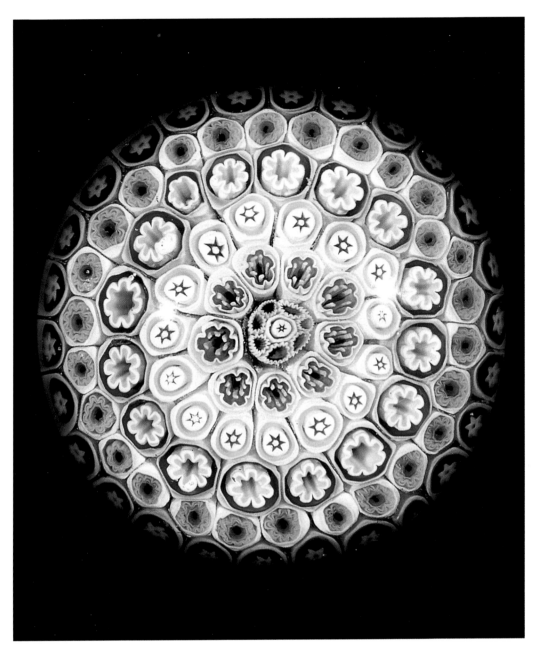

A Bacchus concentric, 1848–55
*The circles of this concentric (**left**) are rather awkwardly set around the central cane. In all but the best examples, Bacchus concentrics lack the formal precision of their French counterparts.*
Diameter: 3⅜in (8.6cm)

A Bacchus ruffle cane.

made, any dated canes. Occasionally, a silhouette cane featuring a lady's profile appears.

Bacchus mainly produced millefiori paperweights. The millefiori canes are much larger than those used in the Baccarat, St Louis and Clichy weights. The colours used are much paler and more insipid than in the French counterparts. Bacchus also produced patterned millefiori weights, in which clusters of canes were formed into circular, square or triangular groups. Identical canes are used within each cluster, although each cluster might consist of canes not contained in any of the other clusters.

Concentrics were popularly used by Bacchus. Usually, five rings of canes fill a large part of the glass to create the illusion, when viewed from above, that they fill the whole of the glass dome. The crimped cane is the most popularly used, but star and ruffle canes are also seen. Mostly the canes are regularly set to give an even, carpet effect that rivals the best of French craftsmanship. However, the canes themselves are not used with the same formal consistency that distinguishes concentric weights made by Baccarat, Clichy and St Louis. One or two erratic canes exist, interrupting the geometry of the design. It is impossible to know whether this feature is intentional or not. However, partly due to their comparative rarity, Bacchus concentrics compare favourably in value with those of the three great French factories.

The heads in Bacchus mushroom weights are always concentrics, while the actual weights are some 3¾in (9.5cm) in diameter. Around the stem of the mushroom is a torsade, usually in vivid colours which are totally uncharacteristic of Bacchus, such as bright pink or blue-green and white. One Bacchus mushroom has been recorded with a torsade and with printies with verticle fluting. The weights are quite box-like in profile, with the sides much straighter and the dome much flatter than is usual with paperweights.

NINETEENTH-CENTURY AMERICAN PAPERWEIGHTS

THE IMPETUS BEHIND THE GROWTH OF

AMERICAN PAPERWEIGHT

MANUFACTURE PROBABLY CAME FROM

THE EXHIBITION AT NEW YORK'S

CRYSTAL PALACE IN 1853. FOR THE

NEXT TWO DECADES, AMERICAN

FACTORIES PRODUCED PAPERWEIGHTS

WHOSE DESIGNS ARE BASED ON THOSE

OF THE GREAT FRENCH FACTORIES.

INDEED, MANY OF THE GLASS-MAKERS

EMPLOYED BY THE AMERICAN

FACTORIES WERE EUROPEANS WHO

HAD ALREADY ACQUIRED THEIR

PAPERWEIGHT-MAKING SKILLS IN

FRANCE AND BRITAIN.

NEW ENGLAND

RECRUITING SKILLED WORKERS

FROM EUROPE, NEW ENGLAND WAS

ONE OF THE FIRST PAPERWEIGHT

PRODUCERS IN AMERICA.

THE LAMPWORK DESIGNS

ARE MORE SUCCESSFUL

THAN THE MILLEFIORI.

A New England fruit weight, c. 1860
Five pears and four red berries rest above
a white latticinio basket.
Diameter: 2½in (6.3cm)

The New England Glass Company was founded in November 1817. The glass factory was sited at Cambridge, Massachusetts, and is commonly referred to simply as Cambridge. The company began by making glass lamps, vases and chandeliers for churches. They also produced lots of glass for the export market to the West Indies and South America. From the outset it was a lucrative and flourishing company, although it ceased production in 1888.

New England paperweight-making began around 1850 and continued until 1880. The first dated paperweight was probably made in 1851: only probably, because the date, rather than being a cane, is part of an intaglio based on a medal struck to commemorate the Great Exhibition in London. The fidelity of the intaglio to the original medal is a clear indication that the mould for the intaglio was cast from one of the original medals and so the weight must have been made subsequent to the Exhibition. The weight is hexagonal and the cameo intaglio depicts the double profiles of Queen Victoria and Prince Albert, with the date in Roman numerals (MDCCCLI).

The New England Glass Company recruited a number of their glass-makers from Britain and Europe. François Pierre was one of those, leaving the Baccarat factory to join the New England factory. Born in France in 1834 and trained in the art of glass-making from a very young age, Pierre left France at fifteen and travelled to America to join this highly respectable and enterprising company. However, his time in Cambridge was marred by ill health, and François Pierre travelled extensively to hot and healthier climates with other members of the glass-blowing fraternity. On arriving at these places they would set up exhibitions displaying their work, and would also demonstrate their techniques.

François Pierre also instructed other workers in Cambridge in the art of paperweight-making. Clearly he was a talented man. His main legacies lie in his extensive work with millefiori and fruit, the latter becoming quite a trademark for the New England factory. Indeed some collectors claim that these surpass even the fruit weights made by the acclaimed factories from France. Sadly, however, Pierre died at the age of thirty-eight in 1872.

The general shape of the New England paperweight is fairly square, and the basal rim is quite deep. The sides of the paperweight rise in a steep, rigid way, and the top is broad and flat. Faceted weights can be

A New England upright bouquet, 1850–80
This large three-dimensional bouquet **(right)** includes flowers, fruit and foliage. It is set above a ground of swirling latticinio.
Diameter: 4in (10.1cm)

A New England flower, 1850–80
This stylized flower **(left)** resembles a camomile or pompom and rests above five green leaves and swirling latticinio. The sides are cut with printies and the top with petal-cuts.
Diameter: 2⁵/sin (6.7cm)

found as can fluting and printies. The quality of the glass is not as clear as in the French weights, and a slightly pinky grey tinge may be detected. The weights are also, like those of Bacchus, very heavy. Usually they are not dated, but there are several known to bear dates. The date 1851 appears on the Victoria and Albert intaglio weight, as described earlier; most of the other weights are dated 1852, although there is record of a millefiori paperweight dated 1854.

The colouring of New England weights is varied and includes yellow, green, pink, orange, blue, purple, white, black and mauve. Each of these colours appears in a variety of shades. The canes are, however, rather uneven at the bottom. There are also figure canes, including the bee, running rabbit, dog, eagle and heart. There are a number of flower weights—the poinsettia, clematis and buttercup—and also flat bouquets. Included in this category is an unusual design featuring a cross of leaves. These last weights are very rare. The leaves are pale green, or else appear as mauve and white petals, with a cane or flower cane placed at the point where the petals cross. They are always found lying on a swirling latticinio ground.

The clematis and poinsettia are also rare and are found in pink or mauve, again resting on a swirling latticinio ground. The leaves are a sure way of identifying the weight as being from the New England factory: they are bright green and the spine and veins are shown, the tip of the leaf being pointed and the bottom being fairly bulbous. Air bubbles on the leaves are a deliberate feature, intended to depict dew drops.

New England buttercups do not bear that close a resemblance to the actual flower, although they do not fall into the stylized category. It would be forgiveable to mistake these buttercups for tudor roses. New England buttercups rest on latticinio or jasper grounds.

The flat bouquets are similar to the St Louis flat bouquets. The bouquets are less languid and are usually comprised of three flowers, with either two or four leaves. These may be found in the average-sized paperweight or else in miniature form.

Some of these weights are faceted, either with circular or oval printies which are sometimes accentuated with vertical fluting. The top is cut with a single printy. Alternatively, there can be one or more four-leafed printies cut into the top, with the printies overlapping one another when there is more than one. In the

A New England intaglio, 1850–60
This hexagonal, clear glass weight **(right)** contains a design cast from a medal celebrating a treaty made with American Indians.
Width: 3⅝in (9.2cm)

A New England overlay, 1850–80
The opaque white overlay **(below)** encases a broad-stemmed, spaced millefiori mushroom. The weight is cut with circular printies and with trefoil, quatrefoil and diagonal facets.
Diameter: 3¼in (8.2cm)

really splendid examples there can be found a central circle of rabbit canes; however, these canes are often somewhat indecipherable and may not always enhance the weight that much.

Overlays exist, but not in abundance. Usually they embellish upright and flat bouquets as well as mushrooms, the colouring of the overlay being a deep, rich red over white, with extravagant cutting to the glass. However, simpler cutting and calmer colours can also be seen. These weights are occasionally dated.

The crown weight is smaller than those made by St Louis and is one of the most successful of the New England weights. There is more clear glass showing around the edge of the crown than in the French weights. The filigree twisted ribbons are not always white, but are sometimes pink or blue. One example shows an all-white twisted ribboned filigree crown; another has a rabbit as the centre cane, with the crown swirling around the inside of the glass horizontally as opposed to vertically. This weight is unique among the output of the New England or, indeed, any other factory.

There are carpet grounds, too. These are rather dull in comparison to those made by the Baccarat and St Louis factories. They consist of simple, short crimped canes with a leaping white rabbit as the central cane.

Concentrics made by the New England factory appear in three varieties: open, closed, and spoked. The open concentric consists of clusters of four canes interspersed in a circle, with a central cluster and also the odd cane placed strategically between the clusters. The canes lie on opaque white latticinio over a translucent red or green ground similar to that of the Clichy factory. Some of these weights are faceted with printies. The closed concentrics are quite rare, are about 2½in (6.3cm) in diameter, and form a typical concentric pattern: a central concentric formation with radiating circles of star-shaped canes. The bottoms of the canes are uneven and not altogether successful. Some examples of this weight are also faceted.

The design of the New England spoked concentric is not very clearly delineated. A number of individual canes are carefully placed at relatively even intervals to set off the design, giving the appearance of a star or spoke. The concentric formation itself is not particularly ordered, unlike the other concentrics, and although the design is not entirely successful it is

*A New England sulphide,
c. 1851
The heads of Abbot and
Amos Lawrence are cast in
profile in this weight (left).
The brothers founded the
town of Lawrence,
Massachusetts.
Width: 3½in (8.9cm)*

*A New England stylized
flower, 1850–80
The white flower (below)
rests on four green leaves
above a white latticinio
ground and is encircled by
two rows of canes. The
weight is cut with printies,
quatrefoils and fluting.
Diameter: 2⅝in (6.7cm)*

nonetheless quite interesting, and very collectable, given its rarity.

The mushroom weights are rather grand in comparison to those of some of the other factories, although not many of these were made. However, it is arguable that the grand design belies a certain lack of refinement. New England mushroom weights have a distinctive large, flat head representing the hat of the mushroom, which is decorated either with millefiori canes or with a flat bouquet with leaves. The glass dome is decorated with a coloured overlay of soft powder blue and off-white and detailed faceting.

Scrambled weights are crammed full of colourful scrambled canes, and may also include parts of the New England fruits. The conventional fruit weights are not a highlight of this factory: most are fairly crude, although some good examples do exist. The most common New England fruits are apples, pears and quinces, lying in opaque white latticinio baskets. The whole design is set in clear glass.

However, although the traditional fruit weights produced by the New England factory are not exciting, there are some very fine and interesting blown fruits which are set on a base. These are not, in the strictest sense, paperweights, since there is no encasing and magnifying crystal dome. The fruits are life-sized and the base is fairly flat and thin. The bases are usually round, although they are also occasionally square. The fruit is blown from clear, opaque glass, and the formed fruit is then dipped with the correct colours according to the variety of fruit. The colours are very accurate and realistic and are mottled, too, to enhance the effect even more. There is even an example of a roughened surface on a peach to give the true effect of its skin. It is important to note that although New England is well known for being the best at producing these fruits, they were far from the first: similar glass fruits were in fact being made in 1714 in Murano and examples from the eighteenth century can be seen today at the *museo* in Murano.

Finally, New England also made a number of intaglio, medallion weights. These are hexagonal, clear glass weights in which the design is pressed into the base. In addition to the Victoria and Albert commemorative weight mentioned earlier, the designs include the heads of Abbot and Amos Lawrence in profile, and one struck from a medal celebrating a treaty made with American Indians during the 1850s.

SANDWICH

A Sandwich stylized flower, 1852–80
This ribbed red and white flower resembles
a double clematis.
Diameter: 2¹⁄8in (5.4cm)

ENJOYING A FRIENDLY RIVALRY WITH NEIGHBOURING NEW ENGLAND, SANDWICH ALSO INITIALLY RELIED HEAVILY ON EUROPEAN SKILLS—PARTICULARLY THE FINE FRENCH CRAFTSMAN, NICHOLAS LUTZ.

Deming Jarves founded the Sandwich Manufacturing Company in 1825. Descended from a Huguenot family called Gervais which left France (initially for Jersey in the Channel Islands) following the Edict of Nantes in 1685, Deming Jarves was born in Boston in 1790. His father was a specialist in making cabinets, chairs and clock cases. Deming was clearly a bright and intelligent boy. By the age of twenty-three he was a trade representative for the Porcelain and Glass Company, which was eventually bought out by the New England Glass Company, establishing a link between Jarves and New England that was never really broken. In 1823, Jarves's father died leaving him the handsome sum of $25,000, which allowed him to fulfill his ambition of owning and running his own factory. Within two years Jarves had formed the Sandwich Manufacturing Company. The name was shortly changed to the Boston and Sandwich Glass Company, of Sandwich, Massachusetts, although it has always been known simply as Sandwich.

Jarves recruited his glass-blowers from all over the world. He was a fiery man with strong ideas who, due to his zealous ambitions, often upset many of his fellow directors which led to many major fall-outs and dis-

agreements. In 1837 he bought the Mount Washington Glassworks for his son, George. In 1869 Jarves died, leaving a vacancy for someone to take over the company. This was done by Nicholas Lutz, who was originally trained at the St Louis factory in France. Lutz was a well-travelled man, who had worked in several different factories in Europe, including one at Murano.

Lutz worked with the Sandwich Company from 1869 until 1888, when the company closed down. He concentrated mainly on flower and fruit weights. When the Sandwich Company closed, Lutz moved with his family to New Bedford where he joined the Mount Washington Glass Factory. In 1895 he moved again, this time to a glass factory at Somerville, where he worked up until his death in 1904. He was buried at Sandwich. There was an attempt to reopen the Sandwich factory shortly after it closed down, but this was unsuccessful for a number of reasons, most of them responsible for the initial failure, such as too much competition and the high costs of labour and of having materials delivered to the factory, which found itself increasingly isolated.

The shape of the Sandwich paperweight more closely resembles that of Baccarat, than of Clichy or St Louis. The sides of the weight are rounded from the

A Sandwich basket of flowers, 1860–70
The pink, white and yellow flowerheads **(right)** resemble Clichy rose canes. The flowers protrude from a green basket set above white swirling latticinio.
Diameter: 2¾in (7cm)

A Sandwich cube bouquet, 1860–88
The bevel-edged glass cube **(below)** encases a bouquet of roses and leaves tied at the stems with a white ribbon. Embedded in the cube beneath the bouquet is a metal mount.
Width: 1¾in (4.4cm)

A Sandwich rose, 1855–88
Two pink roseheads, a bud and two green leaves are realistically depicted **(left)**. The design is set above a white swirling latticinio ground.
Diameter: 2⅞in (7.3cm)

A Sandwich poinsettia, 1860–88
Three rows of slate blue petals are set above five green
leaves. The middle is speckled with aventurine.
Diameter: 2³/₄in (7cm)

base upwards and the dome is flat. Sandwich, it seems, used flint glass more than it did lead glass in its paperweights. The weights are consequently lighter and the clarity rather blurred.

Although many people believe that Lutz was the first to make paperweights at Sandwich, the factory had, in fact, produced a few scrambled weights prior to his arrival. Only two dates appear in Sandwich weights: 1825 and 1852. Clearly, if 1825 is the year of manufacture of weights bearing this date, then this would upset all received opinion about the origins of glass paperweights, and would pre-date the dated paperweights of Pietro Bigaglia and St Louis by a full twenty years. However, it is possible that this is a

A Sandwich group of fruit, 1852–80
Three ripe pears, an apple, a red cherry, a blue plum and
a radish are set in clear glass above seven pointed,
variegated leaves.
Diameter: 2³/₄in (7cm)

A Sandwich weedflower, 1869–88
Attributed to Sandwich, this flower consists of two red
petals above three blue and white striped petals; all are
spotted with aventurine.
Diameter: 2³/₄in (7cm)

mistake by the maker himself, although it should not be forgotten that 1825 was the founding date of Sandwich and is also a transposition of the last two digits of 1852, the likely date of manufacture.

The canes of the Sandwich factory are bright and definite and the use of white is prolific. Figure canes include the bee, running rabbit, eagle, heart and cross. These canes are usually seen as the centre to flower weights, since Sandwich millefiori weights, although produced, are extremely rare.

The flower weights are usually set in clear glass, with or without latticinio and sometimes on a jasper ground. The poinsettia is the most common, with petals in red, light and deep blue, and very occasionally red and blue. Usually the petals take the form of five large petals, with five smaller ones interspersed; leaves and a stem are also included in the design. The quality of Sandwich poinsettia weights ranges from the very good to the very poor. Most of the centre canes are typical of Sandwich (listed above), although sometimes a Clichy-like rose appears in the centre of the flower. These weights were almost certainly made by Nicholas Lutz, who brought the idea and knowledge of the technique with him when he emigrated to America from France.

There is also something called the weedflower, a name which gives very little away. These flowers vaguely resemble the pansy: brightly-coloured stripes

form the three lower petals, while the upper two petals are larger and in a single, bright colour. There is also a stem with leaves. The weedflower is set in clear glass on a coloured ground or on latticinio.

There is also a flower resembling nothing in the botanical dictionary but looking like a cross with two leaves at the bottom. It is set in clear glass, either on a jasper ground or on red-and-white latticinio.

Baskets of flowers also exist, with the flowerheads actually protruding from a wicker-type basket which lies on latticinio. It is interesting that Sandwich chose to do this as it reflects very much the mood of the Victorian age. Jewellery was often designed in this way and these weights are now very desirable pieces to collect, although not at all easy to find.

The upright and flat bouquets attributed to Sandwich are very good, although their provenance is not certain. The uprights are probably better than the flat bouquets, and there is a strong likeness to the equivalent weights produced by St Louis. This is perhaps not surprising, given the background and training of Nicholas Lutz.

Fruit weights appear on latticinio, the fruits not being accurately copied but certainly resembling plums, pears and cherries. Sandwich also made a few blown fruits resting on a flat base, although they are not as good and not as common as those from the New England factory.

GILLENDER

A Gillender carpet ground, 1861–71
The centre of the white carpet ground
contains a silhouette of a woman's head.
Diameter: 3¼in (8.2cm)

THE GILLENDER FACTORY IS NOT FAMOUS FOR ITS STYLE, AND THE WEIGHTS IT MANUFACTURED ARE OF INTEREST PRINCIPALLY FOR THEIR CHARACTER AND THEIR HISTORICAL ASSOCIATIONS.

Originally from Gateshead near Newcastle-upon-Tyne, England, William Gillender was born in 1823. A clever and industrious man, he did not unfortunately live to a great age, dying in 1871. He started work in a glass factory at the age of eight, was lecturing about glass-making at sixteen, and owned a shop by the time he was twenty years old.

Late in 1845, Gillender sailed for America with his wife and family, where he was due to start work for the New England Glass Company. While working there, Gillender was inspired to make paperweights by one of the other workers lured to the factory from France. Gillender soon left Cambridge, however, and worked for a number of glass factories before buying his own factory, known as Gillender & Sons, in Philadelphia in 1861. William Gillender died ten years later and the factory was taken over by his sons, James and Frederick.

In 1930, the factory in Philadelphia closed down, but James Gillender's three sons had already acquired a glass-making factory at Port Jervis, New York, which

traded under the name of Gillender Brothers. This factory still survives.

The early Gillender weights are highly domed, bulbous, and quite wide at the bottom. They are usually cut with six oval printies on the side of the weight and a circular printy on the top. Sometimes, flutes are cut between the printies. Most of the canes are crimps and ruffles, but stars or spokes are also found. The canes are cool pink, cobalt blue, rich aquamarine, mauve and white. The only silhouette cane features the profile of a woman, and occurs in deep loden green, black or white. The silhouette is not thought to portray anyone in particular.

The weights made by Gillender are not usually very exciting. The factory made concentrics, carpet grounds, and a few flower weights. Many of the concentrics are made up of rather mis-shapen canes and with circles rather poorly executed, although there are also some very sophisticated faceted examples. Perhaps the best Gillender weights are the flowers, the finest of which were almost certainly made by William Gillender himself.

A Gillender intaglio, 1875–90
This clear glass weight contains an acid-etched intaglio portrait of Abraham Lincoln. Politicians, religious leaders and the British royal family were popular subjects in sulphide and intaglio paperweights.

A Gillender commemorative, 1876
Above the amethyst base sits a translucent glass model of the Memorial Hall, where the Centennial Exhibition in Philadelphia was held **(below)**. *The model was cast from a mould.*
Length: 6¹⁄₈in (15.5cm)

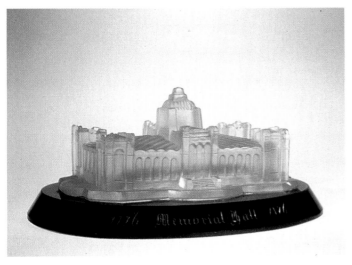

Later on, after William Gillender's death in 1871, the company started to make a number of clear glass weights, many of which featured portraits of American statesmen such as Washington, Franklin and Lincoln. The portraits are intaglios, although, after the design had been pressed into the glass, details were often added or clarified by acid-etching.

In 1876, Gillender made a number of clear glass, moulded weights to commemorate the Centennial Exposition in Philadelphia. These took the form of buildings, animals and birds, and, although they serve a decorative and practical purpose as paperweights, they lack the charm and wonder of classic paperweights, since the glass is no longer being used to magnify an intricate and colourful internal design.

MOUNT WASHINGTON

Mount Washington strawberries, 1870–90
Five ripe strawberries and blossom are
placed above pale green leaves.
Diameter: 4¹⁄₈in (10.5cm)

MOUNT WASHINGTON PAPER-
WEIGHTS ARE TYPICALLY MAGNUM
SIZE, USUALLY ENCASING A
LAMPWORK DESIGN. THE FACTORY'S
FOUNDER, DEMING JARVES, ALSO
FOUNDED THE SANDWICH FACTORY.

Mount Washington has a long and compli-
cated history. It was founded in 1837 by
Deming Jarves for his son, George, who
was then a boy of 12. George Deming
died in 1850, when he was only 25 years old, and the
factory underwent many changes of ownership from
that time until 1958, when it stopped trading. Nicholas
Lutz worked at Mount Washington for a time between
1888 and 1895, and it is thought that he made many
of the factory's weights.

The clear glass domes of Mount Washington
weights are generally not of such high quality as those
of the French factories, and imperfections are visible
even to the naked eye. However, this does not significantly affect the value when the weights are otherwise
of fine quality. Mount Washington weights are extremely desirable, and can fetch large sums of money.
The weights are unusually large, generally about
4–4½in (10–11.5cm) in diameter.

The factory is best known for its rose weights.
More detailed than those of the other factories, the
rose is very attractive and one of the great successes of
American paperweight designs. It is essentially represented as a flat bouquet, although not in the true
sense of the word, since the texture of the rose is very
noticeable and is moulded in high relief. Sometimes it
is just the flowerhead that is seen spreading generously
throughout the clear glass, with dark green leaves
and a stem beneath; alternatively, the rosehead is
smaller and more detailed, and includes a bud in
addition to the stem with leaves.

The rose itself, although not totally natural, is a
realistic interpretation and very well done. Most, but
not all, of the roses appear in pink; lavender blue is
also seen, with variegated buds of blue and pink and
also white, coral and yellow. Butterflies are sometimes
added to this ensemble, although unlike those of the
Baccarat factory they feature more incidentally and
dominate the weight less. Blueberries and red or yellow
berries might also appear, mainly above the rose.
Occasionally, printies are cut into the glass, but in a
rather more discrete way than ever seen before.

The poinsettia also features with this factory. It is a
rather attractive weight, only partly resembling the
real flower, with veined leaves surrounding the bloom.
Dahlias are very rare: orange in colour, their many

*A floral plaque, c. 1880
Until recently, the magnificent paperweights in this style (**above**) have been attributed to Mount Washington, but experts now suggest they may be Russian. Only seven examples are known: all depict arrangements of flowers and foliage tied at the stem with ribbon.
Length: 5¼in (13.3cm)*

*Mount Washington flowers and fruit, 1870–90
Three clematis-type flowers, bunches of grapes and cherries are all sprinkled with aventurine.
Diameter: 4in (10.1cm)*

petals are the same as those used for the poinsettia. Leaves surround the bloom and there is a stem.

Fruit and flowers appear in the form of a bouquet tied at the stems. These weights are very attractive, appearing with plenty of variety in colour. The flowers in the bouquet are stylized, and are arranged in a well-proportioned fashion. These weights are extremely rare, however.

Strawberries are fairly typical of the Mount Washington factory, and are seen in the form of fruit, blossom and green leaves, and also as wild strawberries. The fruit is a fairly realistic, wild strawberry colour and the blossom is white. Like the roses, the strawberries are designed in high relief.

Large floral arrangements appear in a clear glass plaque and are truly outstanding. Previously accredited to Mount Washington, it is now thought they may be Russian. The corners and upper edges are mitred and the base is either plain, hobnail cut or frosted. As with the floral and fruit arrangements, the bouquet is tied at the stems with ribbon in one or two colours. Air bubbles and impurities in the glass can be seen with the naked eye. These plaques are heavy, and there are only seven known examples.

MILLVILLE

A Millville rose, c. 1904
This weight contains a pink rose, which is
placed above a stem and base.
Height: 5¾in (13.7cm)

MILLVILLE HANDSOMELY STRADDLES THE OTHERWISE LARGELY BARREN GULF BETWEEN THE CLASSIC PERIOD AND THE MORE INNOVATIVE DESIGNS ATTEMPTED BY FACTORIES IN THE TWENTIETH CENTURY.

The name Millville, like Sandwich, refers to a place rather than a company or factory. Originally sited at Port Elizabeth, in southern New Jersey, the factory was founded shortly after 1800 by a group of Philadelphia businessmen. The factory began by manufacturing green and white glass for pharmaceutical purposes. At the time of most of the paperweight production, the glassworks were located at Millville in New Jersey and were trading under the name of Whitall Tatum & Company.

In 1863, the company had moved to Millville, and paperweights were sporadically being produced. Millville weights are generally not very refined and fall into one of three categories: birds, flowers, and homespun motifs such as 'Remember Mother' and 'Home Sweet Home'.

The bird weights are probably the earliest to have been made by the factory, pre-dating the company's move to Millville in 1863. The bird weights were not made in great numbers and do not represent a specific type of bird. Instead, they show an idealized form, which is depicted in a childlike way. The bird sits on a twig, lying in clear glass against a coloured ground.

A Millville water lily, c. 1910
Six green leaves and six white petals enclose the bright
*yellow stamen (**above**). A very rare weight.*
Diameter: 3in (7.6cm)

A Millville parrot tulip, c. 1900
*The pink parrot tulip (**left**) contains a bright yellow*
stamen and is set above a green stem.
Diameter: 3in (7.6cm)

The flowers made at the beginning of the twentieth century are particularly attractive, especially the water-lilies, the roses and the tulips. All of the flower weights are set in clear glass, although their form is quite different from that of the traditional weights. The style of Millville flower weights resembles the blown fruits on a base made by the New England Glass Company, except that the Millville flowers are encased in glass and, unlike the fruits, are not life-sized.

TWENTIETH-CENTURY PAPERWEIGHTS

A Stankard flower
A realistic depiction of the bloom, bud,
stem, leaves and root.
Diameter: 2³/₄in (7cm)

SADLY, FEW MODERN PAPERWEIGHTS ARE OF THE STANDARD SET DURING THE CLASSIC PERIOD, AND STILL FEWER SEEK TO EXPAND THE BOUNDARIES OF PAPERWEIGHT-MAKING DESIGNS AND TECHNIQUES.

Glass paperweights continue to be made to this day. Baccarat and St Louis, as well as the Scottish glass factories of Caithness and Perthshire, make weights following the patterns and techniques perfected during the classic period of production during the mid-nineteenth century, and have also produced a number of commemorative sulphides. Essentially, however, these weights are nostalgic, imitating old forms rather than innovating new ones.

The Scottish glass-maker Paul Ysart made a number of patterned millefiori weights, and also some depicting flowers (usually single), butterflies, dragonflies and fish. The best of these were almost all made for export to America, and some contain a cane signed 'PY'. Ysart's best weights show a sympathy and understanding of paperweight-making techniques, while still being very much in the tradition established in the nineteenth century. For truly modern paperweights, one has to look to Sweden and to the glass factories of Orrefors and Kosta, whose weights are abstract and geometric puzzles, playing with perspective and the magnification and diminution of forms

seen through printies. Surpassing the achievements of anyone else, however, are the glass paperweights made by the American, Paul Stankard.

PAUL STANKARD

Paul Stankard was born in Attleboro, Massachusetts in 1944. As a child, he moved with his family to Mantua, New Jersey, an area well known for glass-making, and he still lives there today, taking inspiration for his weights from the woodland flowers that surround his studio. Without doubt, the quality and beauty of Stankard's glass paperweights make them the best that are now being produced.

A botanist by training, Stankard's flowers are totally accurate and beautifully depicted. People often find it hard to believe that the entire paperweight is composed of glass, rather than being an actual floral specimen encased in crystal. Stankard began making floral glass paperweights in 1971 and he was immediately recognized as one of the world's leading glass artists. He has developed his own techniques to achieve a marvellous combination of clarity of crystal, range of colour and delicacy of glasswork.

A group of Stankards, 1986
*Blueberries and blossom (**top**), an 'environmental' weight*
*(**top right**), an arbutus with flowers (**above**) and an*
*orchid (**above right**) are shown here.*

From the early clear glass paperweights encasing glass reproductions of botanical specimens, Paul Stankard has developed and perfected some fine and intricate glass upright blocks. These are very successful and quite unique. Not only does he produce wonderful results with his flowers: roots have come to play an increasingly fundamental role in the design. Most recently, Stankard has invented and developed what he refers to as spirits in the underworld, which can be seen crawling around the roots and on lily leaves. These weights combine Stankard's scientific training as a botanist with a more mythic appreciation of the organic power of nature.

From the very beginning, Stankard's work has been of the very highest quality. The design of his most recent work bears testimony to an increasing sophistication in form, content and technique that continues to place him at the forefront of glass artists, and beyond compare in the field of contemporary glass paperweight-makers. Paul Stankard paperweights can be seen in the collections of eleven museums and art galleries in America, at the Hokkaido Museum of Modern Art in Japan, and at the Victoria and Albert Museum in London.

COLLECTORS AND COLLECTIONS

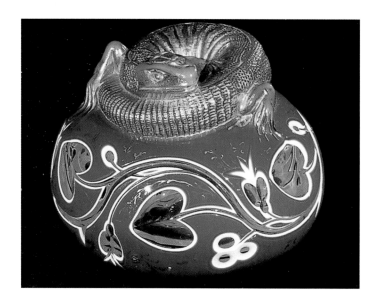

A St Louis mould-blown lizard, 1845–60
The lizard is curled above a green double overlay.
Corning Museum of Glass.
Diameter: 3³⁄₈in (8.6cm)

The role of the collector and commercial market for paperweights first soared to attention with the sale in 1952 of a part of a huge collection of paperweights built up by Mrs Applethwaite Abbott. Although this auction is generally credited as the spearhead for the renewed interest in paperweight collecting, notable collections were also built up by Queen Mary, Empress Eugenie (the wife of Napoleon III), the Marquis de Balleul, Oscar Wilde and, more recently, ex-King Farouk of Egypt. An interesting reference to paperweights occurs in a book written by Henry Green (1905–73), an intellectual, businessman and novelist who was one of the 'Bright Young Things' during his Oxford days in the 1920s. One of the things he mentions about this period of his life in his autobiography, *Pack My Bag*, is an appreciation of paperweights:

Whether we were at fault or not we collected Victorian objects, glass paperweights with coloured posies cast in them, little eternalized baskets of flowers which nothing could break, sometimes they were in the stoppers of bottles, and large piles of waxed fruits under high glass domes rarer because they were the more fragile.

Major collections have also been assembled by highly successful business people, some of whom have been generous enough to leave or loan on a permanent basis their fine and magnificent acquisitions to important, world-recognized museums. Listed below are some of the most significant collections, together with information about the lives of the people who put them together.

The Estelle Doheny Collection at the Edward Laurence Memorial Library was a magnificent collection—one of the most important ever to be assembled— but in February 1988 it was sold by individual lots *in situ* at an auction held to raise money for the St John's Seminary on behalf of the Archdiocese of Los Angeles.

Estelle Doheny was born in 1875. In 1900 she married Edward Doheny, a very rich oil tycoon, who strongly believed that their wealth should be shared

A group of St Louis bouquets, 1845–60
All of the weights contain upright bouquets with gentian-type flowers; the bouquets are tightly grouped in the centre of each weight. The weights formed part of the Estelle Doheny Collection.

and who made generous bequests to many charities.

Edward and Estelle Doheny built up a huge art collection of nineteenth-century European and American paintings, French furniture, Brussels tapestries, European sculpture, Chinese jades, parasols, fans and cameos, as well as a comprehensive collection of European and American paperweights.

Books were their main interest, however, and in 1939, four years after her husband's death, Estelle Doheny financed the building of a library in St John's Seminary, Camarillo. The whole of the second floor of the library contained books solely from the Doheny's collection, which, until its sale in 1988, was one of the finest in the world, with a wide selection of books including a fragment from the Gutenberg Bible.

Upon Estelle Doheny's death in October 1958, the true value of her philanthropy was recognized. Her wishes were that should the Seminary need to raise money then her works of art could be used to help finance and provide whatever was required towards the upkeep and wellbeing of the St John's community. On 3rd and 4th February 1988, the paperweight collection was sold in order to raise money to fulfill the needs of the Seminary and to set up a foundation fund to provide a permanent endowment to the Seminary. So perhaps the circumstances are special for those collectors who bought paperweights from that sale: their acquisitions will be a constant reminder of a most brilliant, thoughtful and generously-inspired patron.

It was fascinating to observe the movement of the market at this time. This auction contained some highly important paperweights, including a rare St Louis orange dahlia weight in clear glass which sold for $19,800. The dahlia has four rows of yellow-ochre petals with brown stripes around a blue and white central cane, with five green leaves, and a star-cut base. It is 2⅝in (6.8cm) in diameter.

A Baccarat blue pompom and bud weight in clear glass, 3⅛in (8cm) in diameter sold for $13,200. The pompom is bright blue with lots of recessed petals about a white star centre. Four green leaves and a green bud show behind, while the stalk has a red bud and three further leaves. The base is cut with a star.

An outstanding Baccarat flat bouquet weight in clear glass, 3½in (9cm) in diameter, sold for $11,000: a central yellow buttercup with a white star centre is surrounded by two blue flowers with arrow's head cogwheel petals and honeycomb centres; by another flower, with red and blue petals, also with a honeycomb centre, and with a pale pink bud shooting over the top; and by white flowers with yellow centres. All of the flowers are surrounded by numerous leaves, and the base is star-cut.

A further flat bouquet from the same sale fetched $13,200. It is 3in (7.6cm) in diameter, set in clear glass, and has an arrangement of three flowers: a blue and white primrose of conventional type and two sty-lized flowers; one red and white, the other blue and white with a dark blue bud, again set among numerous green leaves, the two separate stalks with a leaf on each one. Among the American weights was an outstanding Mount Washington magnum pink dahlia weight in clear glass, 4⅜in (11cm) in diameter. This was sold for $28,600.

The entrepreneur, Arthur Rubloff, without doubt has had a major influence on collectors. A Chicago-based real estate multi-millionaire, he paid the highest price ever realized for a single paperweight: $143,000 at auction for a nineteenth-century weight attributed to the little-known factory of Pantin. He started collecting paperweights in 1947 and gave them as gifts to his partner, who already had a small collection. Rubloff then became a keen collector and started buying for himself, amassing some twelve hundred paperweights over the years. These are displayed permanently at the Art Institute of Chicago.

The Ambassador to France under President Dwight Eisenhower also amassed a large collection of paperweights. His collection was most impressive and comprises a large part of the paperweights on show at the Corning Museum of Glass in Corning, New York. Among these weights is a fine example of a St Louis bouquet with a yellow overlay. It was bought at an auction at Sotheby's in London in 1957 for what was then a world-record price of £3,700. The weight had been a part of the Maurice Lindon Collection, although the sale of many of his weights did not signal an end to his interest in collecting: twenty-two years later, in 1979, Lindon paid what was then a world-record price of $106,000 for a St Louis bouquet with a blue overlay at Christie's, London.

Evangeline Bergstrom (née Hoysradt) was born in 1872 in Ithaca, New York. In 1901 she married her college sweetheart, John Nelson Bergstrom, and in 1904 they founded the Bergstrom Paper Company and the two of them moved from Depere, to Neenah, both in the state of Wisconsin.

Although the papermills were going through extremely hard and difficult times between 1932 and 1934, Evangeline Bergstrom still managed to start her collection of paperweights. She was a religious woman, taking an active role in the First Presbyterian Church of Neenah. The Bergstroms had no children, and consequently Evangeline could abundantly indulge her desire to collect. Having survived the depression of the papermills, as business improved, so too did Evangeline Bergstrom's collection. She was an educated woman who wished to learn more about paperweights and their history, and indeed she built up a very comprehensive knowledge and one of the very best collections ever to be assembled.

Her husband, John Nelson Bergstrom, was highly instrumental in directing his wife's passion for these wonderfully intricate objects, and he undertook to finance the costly publication of her book, *Old Glass*

*A St Louis dahlia,
1845–60*
This gorgeous dahlia
(**above**) was part of the
Estelle Doheny Collection.
The flower has four rows
of yellow-ochre petals
about a blue and white
central cane, and rests
above five pointed leaves.
The base is star-cut.
Diameter: 2⅝in (6.7cm)

*A Mount Washington
rose, 1870–90*
This weight (**above**) is in
the Bergstrom-Mahler
Museum. The design is
packed with detail: a rose,
two buds, fruit and a small
butterfly.
Diameter: 4¼in (10.8cm)

A floral plaque, c. 1880
This paperweight (**left**)
once belonged to Arthur
Rubloff; it is now in the
Corning Museum of
Glass. The weight was
thought to be by Mount
Washington, but may be
Russian.

Two Baccarat weights, 1845–60 These weights once belonged to Estelle Doheny, and illustrate the versatility of Baccarat lampwork designs: a butterfly hovering above the centre of a double clematis (right); and a garlanded butterfly (far right).

Paperweights, one of the most successful and informative books to be written on the subject. (Indeed, the influence of her book was cited by Maurice Lindon of Paris as being the main cause of his increasing his collection. Acclaim for the book was also received from Andre E. Levy of Mexico City, who built up a famous collection of some 600 paperweights.)

John Bergstrom wished for a self-financing museum to be set up on the death of his wife and he made arrangements for a substantial allowance of money to be invested for this purpose. The museum remains unique. John Bergstrom died in 1951 and Evangeline died seven years later. Between the years of their deaths, the town of Neenah accepted as a gift from Mrs Bergstrom her Tudor-style house and its large lakeside grounds as the site for an art centre and museum. Mrs Bergstrom lived in the house until her death, by which time the Neenah Municipal Museum Foundation had been fully incorporated with the Bergstrom-Mahler Museum.

Before the Bergstroms died they made it clear that none of their paperweights or related objects were ever to leave the Bergstrom-Mahler Museum. This was also to apply to any acquisitions that were subsequently made by the collection, using funds from the trust set aside for acquiring more works of art of the finest and rarest quality.

A particularly wide range of thought is expressed in this magnificent collection. Even today, new weights are being purchased, and some outstanding examples of twentieth-century glass-making, including paperweights, can be seen. The museum is also a centre for information and research, and collectors are greatly encouraged to find out more about their acquisitions and the factories that made them.

The Bristol Museum and Art Gallery in south-west England includes some fine paperweights among its exhibits. There are about sixty paperweights on view, mostly from the Baccarat, Clichy and St Louis factories of the nineteenth century. The majority form the Conrad Fry Collection, which was given to the museum in 1940 by Mrs N. L. Cooke-Hurle, a keen collector from south-west England.

Among the weights is a fine Clichy chequered weight, the canes separated by cobalt blue and opaque white ribbon twists. Around this are coiled white filigree threads which are laid between spaced millefiori canes in a chequered pattern, and set on a white muslin ground. A white-and-green Clichy rose and the letter 'C' for Clichy appear.

Another paperweight of note is a fine Baccarat garlanded pansy weight. The crown is cut with six printies, and there is a star-cut base. The pansy has two deep purple upper petals, and three lower petals in dark yellow with purple strips.

There is also a St Louis dated mushroom weight with concentric millefiori circles, within a torsade of twisted white and coral latticinio. It is signed and dated: 'SL 1848' appears in blue and red on white within black, near the periphery.

Among the non-French paperweights there is a mid-nineteenth-century weight from the Sandwich factory in America. This is a five-petalled poinsettia on a white spiral latticinio ground. The flower has a quatrefoil star cane at its centre, and a central stalk with two leaves and two blue buds, each with three

1

2

3

4

5

6

A group of Baccarat flowers, 1845–60
The pansy is the most common Baccarat flower; the one shown here (5) is an unusual early example with lower cogwheel petals. The three camomiles (1, 3 and 6) all display a fine attention to composition and detail. The faceted stylized flower (2) and the double clematis (4) are enhanced by their respective garlands. All of these weights formed part of the Estelle Doheny Collection.

petals. This is a typical example of the weights produced by Sandwich.

A small but very selective and representative collection of antique French paperweights can be found at the Glynn Vivian Art Gallery and Museum in Swansea, Wales. This collection was generously lent in 1959 by Ernest Davies and Dr A. L. Sylvester. The collection includes a fine example of a St Louis snake and a St Louis strawberry and there are some dated specimens, too. The museum also houses an outstandingly good collection of old English glasses.

At the Victoria and Albert Museum in London there is a small but fine collection of antique French paperweights, and also a weight made by the American, Paul Stankard. All of the French weights are from one of the great factories of Baccarat, St Louis and Clichy. These include an unusual faceted upright bouquet made by Baccarat, with a salmon pink torsade, and a bouquet of white, blue and salmon pink flowers; and a very handsome Baccarat carpet ground in pale green with nine silhouettes, which is signed and dated 'B 1848'.

CARE AND MAINTENANCE

MAINTENANCE

Always keep paperweights on a stable surface or in a secure place such as a glass cabinet. Never rest them on a rough surface as this may scratch the base or chip the cutting which has been engraved into the glass. Never allow two or more paperweights to touch or knock together as this may cause ballooning (small or large balloon-shaped globules, depending on how hard the knock is) to appear on the side of the glass.

Never apply anything sharp to the surface of the paperweight. Scratches can be eradicated by having weights repolished, but it is preferable not to resort to this if at all possible: bad workmanship is always a danger, and can seriously affect the value of the weight.

The coloured internal design of a paperweight does not fade under strong light, so there are no restrictions as to where to display them. They can safely be kept in a sunny room without having to worry about fading.

When handling a paperweight, always support it by holding the base, and remove any rings from your fingers that might cause scratching.

CLEANING

Gently rub the surface of the paperweights using a soft, clean cloth, possibly with the addition of a mild domestic liquid cleaning agent.

DISPLAY

Paperweights should ideally be displayed in a well-lit glass cabinet. The best method of viewing them is to place paperweights on angled, clear acrylic stands so that you can see the design easily. However, if it is not possible to place all paperweights on stands choose carefully those that are to sit on the glass, and place them on the lower shelves. Crown weights look magnificent in profile, for example, as do some of the carpet grounds. Upright bouquets also look as interesting and wonderful seen in profile as from above. However, a Clichy swirl, for example, must really be placed on a stand so that the beautifully radiating swirls can be seen to their full advantage.

STORING

When not on display, it is best to keep paperweights in well-lined individual boxes. The lining can be either soft tissue paper or any soft material. 'Bubble-pack' wrapped around individual weights and securely taped is a very satisfactory way of storing weights safely. Never wrap two or more paperweights together.

TRANSPORTATION

Pack up each weight individually and apply storing techniques when transporting. It is absolutely essential to insulate each weight thoroughly.

While occurrences are rare, it has been known for extreme pressure, such as can occur when flying somewhere, to cause the glass to fracture.

PHOTOGRAPHY

Paperweights are extremely difficult to photograph successfully. Great skill is required and it is difficult to find a photographer who can produce excellent results. However, you can achieve very good results yourself if you observe the following useful tips.

Always photograph paperweights individually, using colour film. For the best results, place the paperweight flat on a pane of clear glass about six inches above a light box. Do not use a coloured background as this detracts from the paperweight and causes poor photographic reproduction. Alternatively, if no glass is available, use a sheet of white paper with the light shining up through it. Do not photograph paperweights on stands: reflections often occur, and the edge of the paperweight that is resting on the stand appears mis-shapen, this distorts both the shape and the internal design of the paperweight, and so reproduction is not true to form.

Good lighting is essential. Apart from the light box, there should be a single, overhead source of light. This light should be placed as high as possible above the paperweight, and angled so that it is not directly above the paperweight but rather shines through a cross-section, highlighting the details. Avoid over-lighting, which can reduce the photograph of the paperweight to a silhouette.

Focusing is obviously important in order to achieve a sharp edge to the design. The lens should be focused directly above the centre of the paperweight. It is particularly difficult to focus sharply when photographing magnum weights, which are packed with great detail. Single designs, such as flat flowers or fruits, are the easiest to photograph, since the motif is relatively simple to focus on. With mushroom weights and upright bouquets, it is a good idea to take a second photograph of the weight in profile. This helps to illustrate the full variety and composition of the design.

THE PAPERWEIGHT COLLECTORS' ASSOCIATION

The Paperweight Collectors' Association (PCA) was formed in 1953. Although currently based in Massachusetts, it has members throughout the USA and Canada, and a number in Europe, too. From the very beginning the PCA was enthusiastically supported, and it has grown into a useful and popular way of bringing paperweight collectors together and of sharing information and research.

Members are kept well informed by newsletters, currently sent out five times a year. There is an additional annual bulletin that publishes articles and fine colour illustrations of paperweights. Above all, there is a huge biannual convention which takes place at a different venue each time, always carefully chosen to be near a museum that houses paperweights and related objects. The convention takes place over three days and is very intensive, but very cordially organized and conducted. There are plenty of opportunities for collectors to meet one another, and there are trips to the local museum as well as lectures with slide shows given by well-informed experts. International dealers —mainly from America, Britain and France—take paperweights to the convention to sell, and are always happy to meet and talk to collectors.

Membership of the PCA is not expensive, and the organization is run on a very friendly basis. For information about current membership fees and further details you should write to:

The Paperweight Collectors' Association
PO Box 1059
Easthampton
MA 01027
USA

GLOSSARY

ANNEALING: *A process of reducing the temperature of the completed glass paperweight to make sure that fracturing does not occur.*

ARROWHEAD: *A cane with an upward-pointing arrow design.*

AVENTURINE: *Coloured glass containing tiny crystals of gold or copper to give the effect of a soft and shiny surface.*

BASE: *The bottom of a paperweight.*

BASKET: *A latticinio ground to set fruit or flowers in, or a striped or plain casement of staves resembling a basket.*

BOUQUET: *An arrangement of natural or stylized flowers, with leaves. Sometimes the bouquets are laid flat and sometimes they are upright.*

BOUQUET DE MARRIAGE: *An arrangement of white canes set among a mass of millefiori formed to resemble a mushroom.*

CANE: *Long thin stretched pieces of coloured glass rods which have been moulded together and cut to uncover the internal, cross-sectional design.*

CARPET: *A condensely arranged set of canes.*

CHEQUER: *A paperweight resembling a chequer board. The canes of a scattered or spaced millefiori are separated by twisted latticinio of alternating colours.*

CLASSIC PERIOD: *The height of paperweight production in France between 1845 and 1860.*

CLEAR GROUND: *A clear glass ground.*

CLOSE-PACK MILLEFIORI: *Millefiori depicted in the truest sense of the word: as many canes as possible closely packed together.*

CLUSTER: *A collection or gathering of similar canes.*

COLOUR GROUND: *A coloured glass ground.*

CONCENTRIC: *A very common design: a series of concentric circles of canes radiating from a centre cane (or canes).*

CROWN: *An alternately- or single-coloured weight of twisted ribbons radiating from a central cane, rising to the dome of the glass and running down to the base, filling most of the space inside the glass. Typical of St Louis.*

CUSHION: *A paperweight that takes the form of a pin cushion.*

DATE: *A millefiori cane with a date inserted into it.*

DOME: *The form of glass above the internal design that makes the shape of the paperweight.*

DOUBLE OVERLAY: *A paperweight encased with a thin layer of opaque white glass and then opaque coloured glass. The weight is cut with printies so that the white overlay frames each of the printies.*

ENCASED OVERLAY: *An overlay paperweight, itself encased by an extra layer of transparent glass.*

END-OF-DAY: *An accumulation of canes in a paperweight made up from the remainder of the coloured canes left by the glassblowers at the end of their day's work.*

FACET: *The cutting of glass in a concave manner, similar to that found on gems.*

FILIGREE: *A bundle of twisted opaque white canes, similar to muslin and lace canes.*

FLASH: *A thin layer of transparent glass. Examples of this can be found in the form of an overlay or a flash can be applied solely to the base.*

FLORET: *A single cane resembling a stylized flower head.*

FLUTE: *A deep narrow groove cut into the base of the glass or between printies.*

FOOT: *A piece of glass applied to the bottom part of the paperweight.*

GARLAND: *A chain formation of canes intertwined to form a garland effect.*

GROUND: *A surface towards the base of the weight, above which the design is set.*

HOBNAIL CUTS: *V-shaped cuts on the base of a paperweight, resembling a hobnail.*

HONEYCOMB: *A millefiori cane resembling honeycomb.*

HONEYCOMB FACETS: *Cuts in the glass taking the form of a honeycomb.*

GLOSSARY

INCRUSTATION: *A sulphide in clear glass.*

JASPER GROUND: *An extremely fine-grained ground comprising two colours to form a slightly speckled effect.*

LACE: *A bundle of twisted opaque white canes resembling lace.*

LATTICINIO: *Fine threads of twisted or latticed glass, usually white but sometimes coloured. It is used as a decorative feature, usually in paperweight grounds or torsades.*

MACEDOINE: *A jumble of canes put together. Also known as an end-of-day or scrambled weight.*

MAGNUM: *A very large weight over 4in (10.1cm) in diameter.*

MILLEFIORI: *Probably the most used term in paperweights. Literal meaning (from the Italian): a thousand flowers. A glass-making technique dating back to the second century BC and revived by the Venetians. It provides the basis for the most typical paperweight designs: coloured glass canes are cut to reveal their tiny designs in cross-section.*

MINIATURE: *A small weight measuring 2in (5cm) or less in diameter.*

MOSS GROUND: *A ground of closely-packed green canes comparable to moss. Small white star canes with pink centres can be found sprinkled among the other canes.*

MUSHROOM: *An accumulation of millefiori canes formed in the shape of a mushroom. The canes are brought in at the bottom, spreading out at the dome to resemble a mushroom. The stem is often striped.*

MUSLIN GROUND: *A spiral of twisted opaque white canes, which form the base to some millefiori paperweights.*

OVERLAY: *A paperweight that has been dipped into opaque coloured glass and then cut with printies.*

PAPERWEIGHT: *A decorative glass object of rounded form.*

PASTRY MOULD: *A cane that takes the form of a pastry mould with deep and well defined edges.*

PIERDOUCHE WEIGHT: *A paperweight with a foot.*

PONTIL MARK: *A rough mark on the base of the weight where the pontil rod used in its making has been broken away.*

PRINTY: *A circular or oval concave window cut into the surface of the glass.*

ROCK GROUND: *A ground of granular glass fragments, sometimes seen with green glass chips and mica flakes. It is often the base to Baccarat snake and lizard weights.*

ROD: *A very thin stick of clear or coloured glass. A number of rods are heated up and combined to form canes.*

SCRAMBLE: *A jumble of canes encased in clear glass to form a paperweight.*

SILHOUETTE: *A cane whose cross-section illustrates the tiny detail of an animal or figure in silhouette.*

SPACED MILLEFIORI: *A paperweight which has canes scattered symmetrically throughout the design.*

STAR-CUTS: *A form of cutting seen at the base of the paperweight. It can be found in different sizes, and the star consists of five or more points.*

STARDUST GROUND: *A ground of condensely arranged canes featuring tiny star-shaped dots.*

STRAWBERRY-DIAMOND CUTS: *Cuts to the base of a paperweight at right angles to each other which form a fine grid.*

STAVE: *A basket-like enclosure used in millefiori weights.*

STYLIZED FLOWER: *A flower formed in the manner of a natural flower but not assigned or associated with a particular species. Stylized flowers occur singly or in bouquets, as flat designs and as uprights.*

SULPHIDE: *A ceramic relief incrusted in the glass, often taking the portrait of a famous person.*

SWIRL: *A two-coloured weight formed like a pinwheel radiating from a central cane or group of canes. Very typical of the Clichy factory.*

TORSADE: *A twisting 'ribbon' revolving around the central design in filigree or fine bands.*

TREFOIL: *A three-leafed design typical of Baccarat paperweights.*

WHORL: *An open-ended spiral cane.*

BUYER'S GUIDE

Most people build up a collection over a period of time, budgeting carefully and learning from inevitable mistakes. If you have yet to start a collection, it is worth spending time visiting museums, galleries and auction viewings to familiarize yourself with the range, in quality and design, of paperweights. You may be surprised by how quickly you learn to distinguish the excellent from the average. If you visit the collections at the Art Institute of Chicago, the Bergstrom-Mahler Museum or the Corning Museum of Glass, for example, you should remember that many of the finest exhibits are unique, and that examples of this quality seldom come on to the market.

At auction house viewing days you will learn to gauge which weights fall within your price range, and, of these weights, which most appeal to fill gaps in your collection. The catalogue for the auction will contain full description for all the paperweights, price estimates and many illustrations, so that you will be adding to your knowledge and experience all the time. Once the auction has taken place, a Price List is compiled showing the final purchase price of each lot. Remember that most auction houses add a buyer's premium of ten percent to the hammer price.

Buying at auction, especially for the novice, can be a nerve-wracking experience. The best way to take the doubt and the stress out of buying antique paperweights is to go to a dealer. Dealer's prices will probably be higher than at auction, since the dealer has to add on a profit margin and has also taken a gamble on how long it may take to sell a particular weight. However, a dealer will provide you with full documentation about any weight that you buy and may also, as you build up a relationship, look out for particular types of weights that you are keen to acquire.

There are so many variables in establishing the value of any one paperweight—condition, size, rarity, quality, provenance and so on—that it would be misleading to attempt to attach a price guide to specific types of paperweight. You would be extravagant to spend a four- or five-figure sum on a paperweight without being sure of its quality, and there is no substitute for experience in learning to distinguish between the average, the good and the excellent. However, as an investment, it is always worth buying one or two weights from the top end of your price range rather than five or six examples of poorer quality. The following should be of some guidance to the trends in paperweight prices if you are beginning a collection.

NINETEENTH-CENTURY FRENCH PAPERWEIGHTS

Paperweights made by Baccarat, St Louis and Clichy during the classic period form the obvious basis for most collections. You may decide to concentrate on weights from a particular factory or of a particular design, but you will almost certainly find, at least to begin with, that prices mean that you choose very carefully.

BACCARAT

Pansy weights are quite commonly available, and average to good examples can be bought at auction for £300–400 ($495–660). Other flower weights are rarer, and proportionately more expensive. Auctions at Christie's, London in November 1988 and May 1989 realized hammer prices of between £480 ($792) and £1,100 ($1,815) for double clematis paperweights and £450 ($742) and £600 ($990) for camomiles. Baccarat millefiori weights that are signed and dated are quite common for 1847 and 1848, and although the signature increases the value, it is unlikely to do so as much as for equivalent signed and dated St Louis paperweights. Close-pack and spaced millefiori from Baccarat sold at Christie's London in May 1989 for hammer prices between £450 ($742) and £700 ($1,150), although prices can go much higher. Assuming that they are in good condition, 'bouquets de marriage', overlays, flat bouquets and magnums fetch four-figure prices and more.

ST LOUIS

Although St Louis is particularly associated with crown paperweights, these are not cheap. Few examples fetch less than £1,000 ($1,650) and many now realize sums right at the top end of the scale. Many magnum crowns and those containing an unusual combination of colours in the twists easily fetch five-figure prices. Of the flower designs, the clematis probably fetches the least: Christie's, London sold a number at auction in May 1989 for hammer prices around £400 ($660). Camomiles, dahlias, fuchsias, bouquets and various fruits generally sell for at least twice this amount, and prices, as usual, are much higher for truly outstanding examples.

CLICHY

The swirl weights typically associated with Clichy vary considerably in quality. A Christie's auction in May 1988 saw hammer prices ranging between £190 ($313) and £700 ($1,150), while particularly fine examples will fetch thousands. Among millefiori designs, concentrics are probably the most common, but, again, the range in quality, and therefore price, is enormous: from as little as £140 ($231) to in excess of £1,000 ($1,650). One factor in establishing a high price for Clichy concentrics is the inclusion of Clichy rose canes, particularly if they form a complete circle or appear in an unusual colour. Clichy flower weights are rare, delicate and usually of the highest quality; prices of £2,000–3,000 ($3,300–4,950) are not unusual.

A concentric millefiori, 1845–60

PANTIN

Only eleven paperweights are accredited to Pantin, although others, with lesser certainty, are attributed to the factory. It is, therefore, unlikely that many opportunities to acquire a Pantin weight will arise. This partly accounts for the world record price held by the silkworm weight illustrated on page 54. If an accredited Pantin weight should come up for sale, a new world record may well be established.

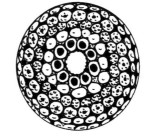

A Baccarat pansy, 1845–60

NINETEENTH-CENTURY BRITISH PAPERWEIGHTS

The range of designs is limited to millefiori paperweights, although quality varies enormously.

WHITEFRIARS

A number of Whitefriars paperweights in the Bergstrom Collection have recently been de-attributed, and it is now thought that they could be Chinese. This may lead to re-appraisal of many weights currently ascribed to Whitefriars—with who knows what effect on prices. Those weights of dubious origin may well fall in value, but with a proportionate increase in the value of those definitely made by the factory.

A St Louis crown, 1845–60

BACCHUS

The rarity of Bacchus paperweights means that they command a consistently good price. It is unlikely that you will find a good example for less than £700 ($1,150).

A Clichy swirl, 1845–60

NINETEENTH-CENTURY AMERICAN PAPERWEIGHTS

The prices of American paperweights are generally high: comparatively few were made; fewer survive; and there is an eager market for them, especially in the U.S.A. As you will see from the examples illustrated on pages 67–81, designs range from the simple and crude to the ambitious and stunning. The former may cost as little as £200 ($330), but most examples now fetch in excess of £1,000 ($1,650).

A clematis on latticinio, 1845–60

INDEX

Page numbers in *italic* refer to the illustrations